# GOD-MINDED

## LIVING GOD-FOCUSED IN A ME-FOCUSED WORLD

*Britney Renae Thompson*

FOR THE MASTER CREATOR,
WHO CALLED ME
TO DO THIS WORK
BEFORE I KNEW I COULD.

# GOD-MINDED

## LIVING GOD-FOCUSED IN A ME-FOCUSED WORLD

*Britney Renae Thompson*

## A NOTE FROM THE AUTHOR.

Thank you for reading God-Minded: Living God-Focused in a Me-Focused World. I believe that the principles in this book have the ability to change your life. Learning the importance of living a God-Centered and God-Minded life will help you step fearlessly and passionately into your God-calling. You were created to live a life full of passion and purpose. Don't ever forget it!

You have taken the first step towards becoming the person God created you to be. It's a journey that God desires for us to take, but so often we become crippled by the fear and doubt that life brings. It's time to drop the unrealistic expectations and lists of impossible standards and live the life of freedom God's word promises to those who have put their trust fully in Jesus.

 See you on the other side!

*Britney Renae Thompson*

P.S. If you are interested in getting to know me a little more you can find me on Instagram and Facebook. I try to respond to each and every individual personally. @britneyrenaethompson

P.P.S. If you get to the end of this book and want more teaching and one-on-one coaching I have great news for you! **I am launching an online coaching course for God-Minded in the spring of 2020!** To receive an invitation to the course launch please visit: www.britneythompson.com and join the waiting list.

**For a list of upcoming events**, or to hire me to speak at your next event go to: www.britneythompson.com.

# FOREWORD BY NAOMI RHODE

*"You are today where your thoughts have brought you, you will be tomorrow where your thoughts take you."*
*James Allen*

Packing in my closet, in Phoenix, Arizona for a 3-week speaking trip to Mackinaw Island, Chicago and New York was a joy! At the pinnacle of a 40-year professional speaking career, I was scheduled for two black tie events, a western theme party, speaking for 60, then 600, then 2000, in those 3 places. The 'Privilege of the Platform' was my calling, my purpose and my passion. That afternoon, however, I felt very sick and spent the evening at the Scottsdale Mayo Hospital ER; but I was assured we could still leave the next morning for this wonderful speaking trip.

Flying was usually a time to read and to rest, watching the world go by below, and this day I was also thinking and praying about the privilege of speaking at the beautiful Grand Hotel on Mackinaw Island. The smaller plane from Chicago to Traverse City, Michigan was a rough ride, though, and the feeling of 'I am not well' returned over and over, though I tried to block it out of my mind. Finally on the ground, Jim went to get the luggage while I greeted our host, a dear friend and client. He gave me a welcoming hug, but as I attempted to hug him back, my arm went limp, my face fell, and my leg collapsed. I said, "I think I am having a stroke' - and I was!

I was unable to walk and had one paralyzed vocal cord (and

still do, which is interesting for a professional speaker). Both my eyes were facing left, the diagnostic nudge that told doctors I had had a Wallenberg Syndrome Stroke. The left vertebral artery had disconnected in my brain, something that happens, sometimes, in football players. I am NOT a football player, so the 'how' is left for eternity to discover. Only 1% of strokes are Wallenberg Strokes, and they are 80% fatal. Needless to say, there was much concern for my life, and then for my recovery.

At one point in the ER, I felt myself lift off the bed. I was up near the ceiling, looking down on my body! Surreal indeed! Hmmm, is this what it is like to go to be with Jesus? I said to Him (out loud), "Either take me up, or put me down; just please stop the room from spinning!" Slowly, slowly, I was lowered back to my body, my life, a loving husband, a mission (to take Christ into the marketplace, the secular world), my three children, and my twelve grandchildren (and now, three great grandchildren). Yes... truly amazing, my God!

Was I afraid? NO! Providentially, I was totally at peace. It was an amazing experience! An Infinite God would care to be in THIS room with ME! An Infinite God would care to give me confidence, confidence in HIS presence, and to give me total peace! I have never had more peace in all my life! Total peace...and partly because I said this verse hundreds of times *"Naomi, God has not given you the spirit of fear, but of love, power and a sound mind (self-discipline)"* 2 Timothy 2:7.

I was in that hospital for 30 days.

We are told that we make approximately 2,000 choices every day. From the simple ones - "Which earrings should I wear today?" or "What should I have for breakfast?" to the complex choices - "How will I *think* today about myself, my mission, my choices, my place in His precious plan?"

Because, dear ones, "As a man *thinketh*, so is he." (James Allen) And, then, I love Frances Schaeffer's challenging statement - it swirls in my head daily - "*How then shall we live*"?

Wheeled into therapy at 9:00 each morning, I would be hanging over the left side of the wheelchair, unable to sit upright. Not a pretty sight! I decided one day I did NOT want Jim to be wheeling me around that way for the rest of my life. Just does not look good! ("Vanity, Vanity, all is Vanity"!) My **choice**: to fight!

It has been said in many ways, "It is not what happens to you, but what you do ABOUT WHAT HAPPENS TO YOU, that makes all the difference."

I COULD **CHOOSE** TO BE BETTER…BETTER EVERY SINGLE DAY!!

I could **choose** to take daily physical, vocal, and hand coordination therapy seriously. Hour after hour after hour! I struggled to put pegs in those little holes, to move my voice from a monotone to a different pitch. And then one memorable day I was told, "You will take a step today!" How do you 'take a step'? How do you get your brain to work for you, to tell your legs and feet what to do? I was learning about the power of my will and my brain, working with HIS will for my life!

A huge motivation for that **choice** (besides vanity) was a precious young Christian woman, with an 8-year old son, who was in the room next to me. She had been in the back seat of a car without a seat belt, and she was thrown through the front window in an accident. She was now a quadriplegic. They would wheel her in for her 9:00 therapy, and she would look at me kindly and say, "Oh, Naomi, how are you today? I woke several times in the night and prayed for you." Humbling to say the least. I had the CHOICE to rehab far beyond her CHOICE, and yet she was the one praying for me!

I *made up my mind and heart* to do my best every single day for His glory! I was in therapy for most of 1 year, to be able to walk, to talk (even sing again), and to continue to fulfill the call on my adult life, my purpose and passion to take Christ into the secular world...AND, to be a great wife, mother, grandmother, great grandmother, and friend for His glory! To indeed be 'God Minded' as the author of this amazing book, Britney Thompson, so clearly and amazingly - even scientifically! - points out and lives out!

Amen, and Amen...you go, Britney...we need to hear your words, in our hurting hearts and conflicted minds!

Do you know Jesus? When life is great, when life is difficult, when choices need to be made? Do you know Him personally as Lord and Savior? I pray you do, or will today! It is the MOST important choice you will ever make!

He knows YOU personally, everything about you. He cares, calls, and counsels you to His perfect will for your life. We are told to fill our minds and hearts with that amazing miracle, and **choose** to live fully, abundantly, mindfully, to His glory, every day!"

May you be blessed by this amazing book.
May you discover the power of your mind to truly be *God-Minded*!

> Naomi Rhode,
> *CSP, CPAE Speaker Hall of Fame*
> Past President: *National Speakers Association,*
> *Global Speakers Federation*
> Co-Founder *SmartPractice*
> YouTube: *Naomi Rhode, Stroke Survivor*

P.S:
Oh, and through this difficult time, God's Sovereignty became truly REAL to me also! My Physical Therapist became a believer! And his whole family. A year later when I returned to speak for the wonderful team at Munson Medical Center in Traverse City, Jeff told me he had gone to the church I had asked him to try. Now he and his whole family were believers and members of that church!'

I told Jeff that I would have had the stroke and done the whole thing all over again, if it was only for him!! His reply was immediate and emotional, "OH...NO, Naomi!" "OH...YES, JEFF!" Strokes are temporal, salvation is eternal!

# CHAPTER ONE

# THE LIES
# WE BELIEVE

I sat in my big comfy recliner in my cluttered living room, a half-eaten large pepperoni pizza on my lap. Netflix was asking me if I was still watching—for the third time—and I cried as I stuffed the sixth piece of pizza into my mouth. When did everything get so out of control? Had I always been such a mess?

The thoughts that paralyzed me in that moment ranged from heartbreakingly awful to downright comedic.

*"Eating this whole pizza is just going to make you feel so much better."*

*"If you finish this you are going to DIE tonight in your sleep!"*

*"This is the last time I will ever eat pizza again, so I might as well eat as much as I possibly can tonight. The diet starts tomorrow."*

*"You are such a failure, you fat lazy cow."*

*"How will you ever get a man if you keep treating yourself this way?"*

As the deafening thoughts swirled around in my head, I sat and cried. When did I become this version of me? In spite of my many dreams and aspirations, I still became the version of myself that I had spent years trying to smother. I dreamed of being the successful, married, public speaker, and writer. Instead, I was single, binge watching Netflix, and sitting in my living room completely alone on a Saturday night.

At 32, I was deep in the throes of a 15-year eating disorder and hating myself more and more each day. To add insult to injury, I knew my eating disorder was bringing me one step closer to my grave each time I binged. To the people around me, I was the confident, Godly, happy-go-lucky Britney I had always been; but the facade was beginning to crack. It was time to make a change, but why would this time be any different? I had tried and failed so many times that I had lost count.

If you have ever had a time like I just described, full of irrational, painful thinking, then congratulations...you are completely normal! As I share my story, it is amazing how often I hear parroted back to me a similar saga. For you it may be the inability to stop working out. For another it might be overspending and getting into debt. If you are a young mother, your negative thinking may come from feeling inadequate as a mother. As we struggle with our thought lives, we become convinced that we are the only ones struggling with these issues. But this problem of stinking thinking affects us all unless we get our thoughts under control.

Modern-day culture and philosophy tell us, in order to be happy, we need to look out for number one. In order to do that well, of course we must trust our own feelings and thoughts above anything else. We have been taught that, unless we trust ourselves first and foremost, we can never be fulfilled. Look out for number one; you deserve to be happy all the time. If it's not fulfilling to you, then it's not worth working at. Happiness and fulfillment are the most important things in this life. If something or someone comes along that doesn't make you feel good, then they don't deserve to be a part of your life.

Let me be the first to stomp all over that me-mindedness and tell you that it is completely untrue. God's Word gives us the easy answer to this problem, and it is the exact opposite of the cultural norm. God's Word tells us to work hard at cultivating a renewed mind. Put others above your own happiness and desires. Trust God and His Word and you will become the person you were created to be, even if that means ignoring your desire for personal comfort and satisfaction.

We are being lied to when we are told to trust our thoughts and our emotions. Let me give you an example from my own life. Have you ever awakened in the morning, put on an outfit, and thought, "Man, I am rocking this! I am one hot mama." This usually happens to me about the fourteenth day of my super strict diet. But then for lunch you slip up a bit by eating that chocolate chip cookie (or two) your co-worker brought into the office. Around three o'clock, when the bloat sets in, your thoughts begin to spiral. "I shouldn't have eaten that cookie (or two)...I probably gained 10 pounds. I can't believe I just threw out my entire diet! This outfit makes me look so fat. What was I thinking when I put this on this morning? Oh well! I messed up, might as well keep going and start over again tomorrow." How can we possibly go from "I look so hot" to "I am one fat cow, better eat everything" in just a 6-hour span? It is because our brains are lying to us about the truth to keep us in our normal, crazy cycles.

**Whatever we cultivate in our lives is what will grow. And the longer we let something grow, the more normal that pattern of thought becomes.**

**Titus 3:3-8**

*"At one time we too were foolish, disobedient,
deceived and enslaved by all kinds of passions and
pleasures. We lived in malice and envy, being hated
and hating one another. 4 But when the kindness and
love of God our Savior appeared, 5 He saved us, not
because of righteous things we had done, but because
of his mercy. He saved us through the washing of
rebirth and renewal by the Holy Spirit, 6 whom He
poured out on us generously through Jesus Christ our
Savior, 7 so that, having been justified by his grace, we
might become heirs having the hope of eternal
life. 8 This is a trustworthy saying. And I want you to
stress these things, so that those who have trusted in
God may be careful to devote themselves to doing what
is good. These things are excellent and profitable for
everyone."*

Did you notice the huge difference between the person
being described in verse three and the person we should
become after being saved in verses five through eight? The
reason there is such a huge difference between the foolish,
disobedient, hating slave in verse three and the person in
verses 5-8 should be very evident to us. First, we have
been saved. Second, the Holy Spirit has renewed us and
justified us in the eyes of God. And third, this person is
carefully devoting himself to good works. It is the best
type of cultivation that can happen in the life of a believer.
As believers, we have never been called to be perfect, but
we have been called to the spiritual discipline of renewal.

We hear Christian words all the time, but there is a benefit
to understanding the definition of these words. Many

people use "Christianese" in order to sound, well, more Christian; but seldom do we think about the raw, simple definition of a word. Here is a simple definition in case you are like me and use words when you may not know the full meaning:

### RENEW:

1: to make like new: RESTORE to freshness, vigor, or perfection
2: to make new spiritually: REGENERATE
3a: to restore to existence: REVIVE
3b: to make extensive changes in : REBUILD
4: to do again: REPEAT
5: to begin again: RESUME
6: REPLACE, REPLENISH
(From Merriam Webster dictionary)

Remember this definition as we talk about renewing our minds or mind renewal. This concept has the ability to change all of our lives for the better, yet I only know a few people who put it into practice regularly. As a Christian, I knew that I was supposed to renew my mind; but until a few years ago I had no idea how to practically make that happen. God-Minded will give you a simple and effective solution for you to begin being more intentional about mind renewal.

Before I get into the practical side of renewing your mind, let's focus on the foundation for this biblical doctrine. Take some time to think through these questions.

1. **When is the last time I actively thought about what I think about?**

2. How often do I correct my thoughts?
3. What are the three biggest lies I tell myself on a regular basis?
4. If there was one lie I believe about myself that I could correct or change, what would that be?

Considering these questions will start you on the process to the practice of renewing your mind. It is such a simple practice, yet probably 90% of the people reading this book have never thought through those questions. We may KNOW that we should be renewing our minds, but it's something we put off to the side as something we will do when we have more time.

As I have met with and spoken to hundreds of women, the same lies float to the top. These are some of the biggest lies that women today believe about themselves:

# 1. I CANNOT BE BEAUTIFUL UNLESS I AM THE RIGHT SIZE OR LOOK A CERTAIN WAY.

This belief system is categorically untrue in more ways than one. Did you know that the standard of beauty in magazines and on television is only about 1.5% of the world's population naturally? That means that 98-99% of us do not fit into the world's standard of beauty—and we never will. Here's a crazy thing to consider: if I had lived 100 years ago, I would have been considered a beautiful woman with all of my luscious curves. Beauty standards change and, unfortunately, the standard of beauty in the twenty-first century is unachievable for most.

How many of us have bought into this lie? I would guess that 99 out of 100 women have tried to manipulate their bodies in some way to be more beautiful. The diet industry is projected to be a 72 billion dollar industry this year, and the statistics are that only about 2% of people who start a diet will keep the weight off throughout their lifetime. Let's not even get into Botox, surgeries, and the removal of hair from unmentionable areas! So why have we bought into this deception hook, line, and sinker?

The answer lies in our brains. The current standard of beauty is something that our brain is seeing on a regular basis at every turn. Because of the rise in digital and social media, we see the flashing billboards and ads of what beautiful is all the time. In fact, it is estimated that a person living in the USA will see about 5,000 ads every single day. Although it is no longer difficult for us to get real information about the negative effects of the lying diet industry, we still believe the marketing ads that are targeted directly at us through our news feeds.

As long as we are talking about social media, let's get real. Be honest: who posts an unaltered picture on social media anymore—no filter, no make-up, in not-so-great lighting? Not only are we setting up unrealistic standards for others, we set them for ourselves as well. Our pictures don't even look like us anymore because we think that, in order to look beautiful, we must alter or boost our appearance. I know women who refused to go to their high school reunions because of how they looked. The facade of filters took away their confidence and desire to actually live their life and connect with friends from their past.

Of course, there are things that make me giggle. When I see a very clearly altered picture of a woman with some of the apps applied, I find my mind wandering 50 years into the future. Our poor grandchildren are going to see some of our Snapchat pictures and think what a funny dog grandma was, and wonder when it was that she got her nose and ears removed. But I digress...

We sabotage each other while we are sabotaging ourselves. We are each other's worst enemies. Instead of loving support from the women in our lives, women are known for being catty, backstabbing witches. Who hasn't seen a chick flick recently with one of these characters? Worse yet, who hasn't lived it? Unfortunately, we have bought into the lie that we can only feel good about ourselves when we put other women down. Instead of being one another's friend and advocate, we replace relationship with the need to feel superior to one another. How sad!

Our brain is not naturally good at filtering out things that aren't true unless it has specifically been told to do so. Throughout our day, even when we aren't actively seeking it, we are being told that we are not pretty enough at least 50 times each hour (estimating that 25% of all ads are beauty or diet ads). Although this book doesn't specifically deal with eating disorders or the non-diet movement, it's important because this is an issue that most women in the US will struggle with at some point in their lives.

As a 20-year-old woman, I believed that in order to be beautiful I had to look like that supermodel on the cover of my favorite magazine. All I needed to do was lose that extra 20 pounds and become stick thin. I tried everything from starvation diets, to low carb diets, to high fat or low fat diets. I weighed, measured, and counted points. I even, at one point, injected myself to lose weight the "easy" way. No matter what I did, that 20 pounds just wouldn't stay away! As soon as I would stop dieting, I would gain back everything I lost plus 5 pounds. I began abusing my body so profusely that my brain amped up the mechanism to get me to eat when I just couldn't starve myself anymore.

At the age of 22, I began binging. It was slow at first, maybe once every couple of months; but as the cycle of dieting continued, it worsened. In 2016, I was diagnosed with binge eating disorder and told that I would have to manage my eating disorder for the rest of my life through diet and exercise. To this day, two of my least favorite words on the planet are "diet" and "exercise." They had failed me, and I was angry. I was angry that the very thing that I thought would "fix" me had broken me. I was angry that the diet industry is lying to people about their effectiveness. But, most importantly, I was angry that I had believed that lie for so long.

In 2017, I hired a coach that helped me get rid of my eating disorder through cognitive behavioral therapy. By changing my thoughts about food, I stopped binging and haven't had a problem with binge eating since. It was at this point in my story that I learned the truth about what renewing your mind actually meant. It meant life, and health, and success, and everything that I felt I was currently lacking. God's Word lays out the truth; and as I studied the brain, its functionality, and how to change habits and patterns, I soon realized that the Bible had the answers I was looking for.

**Even though the media is constantly bombarding my senses with the lies of beauty, I no longer believe them. In fact, it no longer has any pull or sway on me at all.** I have learned how to combat those lies with truth. They are no longer allowed to control my mind or my actions.

My prayer for each woman that reads this book is that you would believe the truth of what God's Word says about you and your lasting worth and beauty.

> *1 Peter 3:3,4*
> *"Your beauty should not come from outward adornment, such as elaborate hairstyles and the wearing of gold jewelry or fine clothes. 4 Rather, it should be that of your inner self, the unfading beauty of a gentle and quiet spirit, which is of great worth in God's sight."*

> *Psalm 139:14*
> *"I praise you because I am fearfully and wonderfully made; your works are wonderful, I know that full well."*

> *Proverbs 31:30*
> *"Charm is deceptive, and beauty is fleeting; but a woman who fears the Lord is to be praised."*

## 2. UNLESS I _____, I AM NOT SUCCESSFUL. *(Fill in the blank: Have a family, Have a good job, Go to school, etc.)*

Another huge lie we believe is that of success. The American dream has people searching until the day they die for lasting success and happiness. First of all, success should have nothing to do with superficial things such as jobs or possessions. Those things will never bring lasting joy. Secondly, success should never be chased after at the expense of another human being or your own soul.

For many women I know, their feeling of success comes from the fact that they are as successful—or more successful—than the men in their life. Many women feel they either have to be "under" a man or "over" a man. In reality, men are just people, too. Your value has nothing to do with comparing yourself to a man. You should be paid the same as any other similarly qualified person, man or woman. It's okay to stand up for that. But we don't have to try to be equal to men, just to prove our value; we ARE equal to them and valuable because **we are all God's unique creation.**

But as women we have innate differences, too. Exercising those differences (EX: being a mother and not being willing to work 60 hours a week for a promotion) makes us all the more unique, not less than - or more than - a man. Having confidence in who we were created to be can help us avoid society's trap of comparing and competing with our fellow human beings who are male. Knowing and trusting God's purpose for us can help us avoid participating in the over the top feminist agenda of America in the 21st century.

Instead of trusting what God says about who we were created to be, women search for the world's definition of success in jobs, marriages, possessions, money, and travel. But how many people do you know that get to the end of their life and wish they had spent more time making money, or buying more stuff, or working 10 more hours a week?

Another success lie comes from the unrealistic ideal of perfectionism. For some reason our culture thinks it is okay to stack a pile of endless duties and activities on top of women in order to measure their success. The list includes: juggling a career and family, cleaning their spotless 4,000-square-foot house, extra-curricular activities for kids, ladies' night out, being the perfect wife, keeping up with that blog, eating the perfect diet and keeping the perfect body. How often have you believed the lie that you have to keep the perfectly clean house, with the perfectly put-together family, in order to be successful as a mother?

Over the years I have met AMAZING mothers who believed that they were failing in raising their families and children. In fact, I would venture to say that this might be the biggest lie young mothers face today. (Well, and that they need to get down to their pre-pregnancy weight within a week of giving birth. Who started *that* lie anyway?) I'm sure there are more I am missing, but the truth is that we just can't do it all, ladies. It is impossible to do it all and have that "perfect" life we are told we must have in order to be successful. A lot of this feeling of not measuring up comes from social media and the comparison trap.

What about having a degree or finishing school? Many women I know spent thousands of dollars (usually borrowed) on a degree that they will likely never use. You do need a degree in many professions, but why get a degree you have no desire to use? Young people have bought into the lie that getting a degree ensures a great job making six figures. The truth is that many college graduates are going after the same not-six-figure jobs in a market that may be saturated. Think about your cost/benefit ratio. Are there jobs in the field you are pursuing? Does your dream job even require a degree? Will you be able to pay off that student loan with your real projected income? I have known women who have achieved an ivy-league education to become a school teacher. They now have a $100,000 school loan that they will be paying on for the rest of their lives— when what they really want is to teach for a few years, then start a family, and own a house!

Interestingly, the very things the world tells us will bring us success and happiness may actually draw us away from the things that are worth something. The world's definition of success is empty compared with the things God's Word lays out as true success.

### Psalm 1:1-3
*"Blessed is the one*
*who does not walk in step with the wicked*
*or stand in the way that sinners take*
*or sit in the company of mockers,*
*2 but whose delight is in the law of the Lord,*
*and who meditates on his law day and night.*
*3 That person is like a tree planted by streams of*
*water, which yields its fruit in season*
*and whose leaf does not wither—*
*whatever they do prospers."*

### Proverbs 16:3
*"Commit to the Lord whatever you do,*
*and He will establish your plans."*

*Proverbs 14:12*
*"There is a way that appears to be right,*
*but in the end it leads to death."*

# 3. I HAVE TO HIDE WHO I AM IN ORDER TO BE LIKED.

This is a lie from the pit of hell that is meant to keep you out of the race and to stop you from having an impact in our world. **Who God has uniquely created you to be is exactly who you SHOULD be.** I believed the lie that I had to be liked by everyone for many years, and unfortunately I am not alone. As human beings we crave popularity and love. We don't want to be different, so we spend time and energy creating a different personality that people will like. It is a lie that we start believing when we are very young.

Culture tells us the lie that we need to stand out in some way, to be perceived as different. At the same time, it tells us how we should dress, the things we should believe, and the way we should act in order to be accepted. Any major fashion trend proves that we are *not* actually supposed to be different, according to the world's standards. Seriously, who persuaded us to want to wear parachute pants or leg warmers in the middle of the summer? I recently saw a fashion trend advertised for jeans that literally have clear vinyl over the knees, and people are actually buying them! We are so easily persuaded to do and act a certain way through the use of advertising and media. However, if you dare to take a stand and believe what is not acceptable, you will be labeled intolerant. Our world celebrates different as long as it fits into the acceptable box.

Not only does the Bible teach us that we are meant to be unique and different, but also that we are meant to live with purpose and passion. Our identity is special because a God who doesn't make any mistakes created it. He is the magnificent Potter who made each of us a rare creation of His brilliant imagination. But He also created us to bear His own image in all His unimaginable and spectacular magnificence.

I don't think it's by accident that each person has her own individual fingerprints, or that we are each born with very specific natural talents and abilities. Our identities are so much more than the things we do or don't do. Our identity, when viewed rightly through the Biblical lens, is a beautiful picture of the amazing Creator of the Universe. There is no other living creature on this planet that has the ability to think and reason and grow and learn the same way that human beings do. From birth we are purposefully significant and one-of-a-kind. God created nothing by accident, especially you!

> **Genesis 1:27**
> *"So God created mankind in his own image,*
> *in the image of God He created them;*
> *male and female He created them. "*

> **Jeremiah 1:5a**
> *"Before I formed you in the womb I knew you,*
> *before you were born I set you apart;"*

> **Psalm 119:73, 74**
> *"Your hands made me and formed me;*

*give me understanding to learn your commands.*
*74 May those who fear you rejoice when they see me,*
*for I have put my hope in your word."*

## 4. I AM INSIGNIFICANT; THERE IS NOTHING SPECIAL ABOUT ME.

Culturally, we must be extraordinary to get anyone to notice us. Every day we see people who do amazing things, and we pine after their exciting and perfect lives. Reality TV has made it almost impossible for us to separate what *is* normal from what is perceived as living a "normal," fun, and exciting life. Programs that show beautiful people living a "successful" life while partying all the time and having a different sexual partner every night are completely dishonest and impossible. But that is quickly becoming the new American dream. Live life the way you want until you can't party anymore, and then when you are finished having fun, it is time to get serious and settle down. In the meantime, this confused generation is growing up believing the lie that they are the only ones who feel unsatisfied, empty, abandoned, and used.

We were never meant to live that way! The problem is that we forget that our lives are meant to have the mundane in them as well. We need to have those things that just aren't fun in our lives to keep us grounded and maturing. No matter how much we hate doing our taxes or setting a budget, those are things that that we need to do in order to keep our lives from spinning out of control...or in the case of our taxes, to keep us out of prison. We believe the lie that, because people broadcast their most exciting moments online for the entire world to see, our lives are just boring and inconsequential. Nothing could be further from the truth.

Our significance doesn't come from whether or not our lives are exciting or if we can do or say something stupid enough to get one million views. It doesn't come from our ability to draw a crowd. It doesn't even come from our talents and abilities to create amazing music or works of art. **Our ultimate significance comes from the fact that the Creator of the Universe says that we are significant and loved.**

The lie that says we are not important or that we are of no consequence is similar to the lie that tells us we must look and act a certain way. The thing that makes you the most special is your innate worth that comes from a God who loved you and gave His life for you. It doesn't matter that someone else thinks you are irrelevant or boring because God says that you are wonderful! Your importance comes directly from the God who sent His only Son to die on the cross in your place. How much more significance could we want?

> **John 3:16**
> *"For God so loved the world that He gave his one and only Son, that whoever believes in Him shall not perish but have eternal life."*

> **Psalm 139:13,14**
> *"For you created my inmost being;*
> *you knit me together in my mother's womb.*
> *14 I praise you because I am fearfully and wonderfully*

*made; your works are wonderful,*
*I know that full well. "*

**Matthew 10:30,31**
*"And even the very hairs of your head are all*
*numbered. 31 So don't be afraid; you are worth more*
*than many sparrows."*

## 5. NO MAN WILL LOVE ME UNLESS I LOOK A CERTAIN WAY.

This last lie is specifically for the single ladies out there. This is a lie that I have believed on and off for almost 20 years. It is a lie that is spoken in hurt and hate often and even sometimes spoken from a place of love. But the fact of the matter is that this is a lie no matter how it is spoken. A person's worth should never be presupposed based on their physical appearance.

For many years as I struggled with my eating disorder, that lie was a driving force in my steady decline to obesity. It was my protection—and at the same time, it was my undoing. I desired to be loved and to get married and to have a family, yet past hurts left me unsure if I could ever trust a man in that way again. I hid behind my eating disorder as it gradually became my identity and my defense. I believed, as the lie often says, that if I stayed overweight I would never have to open myself up to that level of hurt again. But what I didn't realize was that I was actually hurting myself more than a man ever could. I downgraded my worth to my weight and let it define and control my life.

This lie is a lie of manipulation. Our culture says that, unless you are beautiful in the eyes of a man, you have no worth, especially if you want to date and marry a good-looking, muscular, and in-style man. Do you see the reverse side of the lie? This lie puts both men and women into the category of worth based on their physical appearance and ability to buy the nicest and best clothing, while at the same time making them slaves to the idea of physical perfection.

**The Bible says that a woman's worth comes from her soul, her innermost being.** When talking about our identity, the Bible never once says that our worth comes from the way we look or how people view us. I would also add that being married is never held up as the standard for our worth anywhere in the Bible. As I have grown in my personal character, I have come to realize that this time in my life is a sweet time to fall more in love with the God who gave His life for mine. And in the process, a surprising benefit is that I grow to love myself to a greater extent as well. Because my significance is found in my Creator, I no longer need to seek acceptance from the people around me.

> *1 Corinthians 7:7,8*
> *"I wish that all of you were as I am. But each of you has your own gift from God; one has this gift, another has that. 8 Now to the unmarried and the widows I say: It is good for them to stay unmarried, as I do."*

> *1 Peter 1:18,19*
> *"For you know that it was not with perishable things such as silver or gold that you were redeemed from*

*the empty way of life handed down to you from your ancestors, 19 but with the precious blood of Christ, a lamb without blemish or defect."*

**Romans 5:8**
*"But God demonstrates his own love for us in this: While we were still sinners, Christ died for us."*

# CHAPTER TWO

# FOUNDATIONS

When I first started the practice of renewing my mind daily, it came from a place of desperation and need. The entire practice felt strange and out of place in my "normal" Christian mindset world. I felt I needed to hide my practice from the people around me to maintain the facade of "normal, Godly Christian" and not "new-age, hippy freak."

As I dove into mindfulness and the Biblical concept of renewing your mind, I quickly found that I had NO IDEA how much information was out there; it was quite honestly overwhelming.

One day I sat in the corner of a coffee shop with my headphones in trying to hide my computer screen from the world as I watched yet ANOTHER video about the importance of mindfulness. The concepts being taught were so weird and unsettling to me! This person was literally telling me that through the process of renewing my mind I would be able to live a more free life and be able to "manifest" anything I wanted. In the middle of a rather compelling argument as to why this was possible in my life, I just couldn't take it anymore. In the Christian circle where I grew up, I was told to STEER CLEAR of those "word-of-faith", "prosperity-gospel" teaching people. I closed my computer screen and put it away, vowing I would give up this worldly thinking of mindfulness, telling myself all I needed was to know that God was in control and He would work it all out.

The funny thing now is that I 100% believe the message I was seeing—just from a much different perspective. While I don't believe that I can manifest anything on my own in my own life, I do believe that God is the giver of all good things and desires to bless us. The Bible is so clear that if God is in control of everything and is sovereign, then He already has those things prepared for me to grab hold of and run with. **The Bible teaches us we were created to live with purpose, and we are called according to God's purpose for us.** I don't believe it is any accident I live in this world, at this moment in time, and in the place where I live. I don't believe it is an accident I grew up in a family with God-loving, theology-passionate parents who taught me to go to God's Word for truth. And I don't believe it is by accident I have a deep longing and passion to share truth with women so they can break free from the lies in their heads. God's desire for you and me is to live according to His purpose by stepping into the calling He has crafted specifically for us. So what are we waiting for?

That question is one that has plagued me for many years. What am I waiting for? Well first of all, I am waiting to be the person I think I NEED to be in order to step into that calling. I am waiting to lose the last 50 or so pounds. I am waiting for someone to SHOVE me through the open door and put me on a stage. I am waiting to meet the right man. I am waiting until there is nothing else to do. Basically, I am waiting for the perfect circumstances to line up with my perfect body and the perfect opportunity. The problem with waiting for perfection is that it NEVER comes. Life is messy and opportunities often present themselves in messy ways. There are always things that will get in the way or stop you from becoming that perfect person. It is just not probable or likely that your God-calling will present itself in any perfect way.

**WHAT IF** God's desire for you is to step into your God-calling in all of your glorious messiness?

**WHAT IF** the waiting is just an excuse to NOT do what you are passionate about and called to do?

**WHAT IF** we only have a short amount of time on this earth, and we are wasting it believing the lie that everything must fall into place perfectly before we finally make our move?

> ### *John 10:10b*
> *"I have come that they may have life, and have it to the full."*

> ### *Matthew 6:34*
> *"Therefore do not worry about tomorrow, for tomorrow will worry about itself. Each day has enough trouble of its own."*

> ### *Romans 8:28*
> *"And we know that in all things God works for the good of those who love him, who have been called according to his purpose."*

Throw out everything you think you know about the practice of mindfulness and meditation. It is probably completely wrong when thinking in the context of God's Word. We are going to build a BIBLICAL foundation of mindfulness, or maybe it would be better labeled God-Fullness. It is the turning from me-mindedness to the practice of God-mindedness.

*Let's lay the foundation.*

# 1. THE MIND AND HEART CONNECTION

In the Bible, the mind and heart are synonymous with one another. More specifically, our mind and heart are our innermost person, our personality, the part of us that makes us uniquely us. The Bible has a LOT to say about both the mind and heart. In fact, the Bible talks more about our heart and mind than any other body part. It tells us that we should be caring deeply for our hearts, above ALL ELSE.

> ### Proverbs 4:23
> *"Above all else, guard your heart,*
> *for everything you do flows from it."*

Proverbs 4:23 is kind of my go-to verse when it comes to caring for our hearts and minds. It is so clear by looking at this verse that *caring for our heart is an intentional ACTION that must be performed.* Our hearts are not merely meant to be looked after with a sidelong glance, but are meant to be guarded. When I hear those words, I instantly get a picture in my mind of a guard posted outside of a locked cell. He stands at attention as he watches and waits for intruders. He holds a weapon that will deter anyone from making a move on the thing he is guarding. Now let's contrast that with how well we actually guard our hearts.

I have heard this verse used time and time again to tell a person not to get too attached romantically to another human being. And that's it. I have only ever heard this verse taught as a call to Godly living one time, at a wonderful church I attended in Phoenix. But overwhelmingly often this verse is taught as an afterthought to a great sermon on choosing romantic relationships wisely and not allowing your heart to get too attached too quickly. While I agree that is important, the context of this verse goes so much deeper than that.

This chapter in Proverbs teaches us how to live with wisdom in a world that is in direct opposition to the message being taught. It outlines not only WHY we must walk in wisdom but HOW to walk in wisdom. As the chapter concludes with a rundown of our bodies and how to live a Godly life, verse 23 is set smack dab in the middle of it all.

### Proverbs 4:20-27

*"My son, pay attention to what I say;*
*turn your ear to my words.*
*21 Do not let them out of your sight,*
*keep them within your heart;*
*22 for they are life to those who find them*
*and health to one's whole body.*
*23 Above all else, guard your heart,*
*for everything you do flows from it.*
*24 Keep your mouth free of perversity;*
*keep corrupt talk far from your lips.*
*25 Let your eyes look straight ahead;*
*fix your gaze directly before you.*
*26 Give careful thought to the paths for your feet*
*and be steadfast in all your ways.*
*27 Do not turn to the right or the left;*
*keep your foot from evil."*

Do you see the urgency in this piece of scripture? The intentionality? Do you see anything about guarding your heart in a romantic relationship? Neither do I. The whole point of this passage is a father teaching a son how to live a life pleasing to the Lord. It was written to teach his son how to live a life worth living in a world that will try to lead him astray at every turn. Interestingly, each verse includes very specific action words. This isn't just a teaching lesson for this son to catalogue away. It is an intentional, fully-immersed call to action in his life. The key verse (in the middle) literally says this. The most important thing you must do is guard your heart diligently, because EVERYTHING IN YOUR LIFE (your emotions, actions, reactions, etc.) comes from that inner man you are cultivating. It is literally the beating heart of your life, the essence of who you are as a person and of every action you will take in your life.

Here is another verse that has the exact same message.

> **Proverbs 27:19**
> *"As water reflects the face,*
> *so one's life reflects the heart."*

Our lives are the outward reflection of our inner heart. When our heart is not,watched after, our lives are out of order. When we ignore the things inside us that are wrong, our lives become a mess.

When I was in my late 20's, I bought a cruise for my sister and myself for Christmas. I was so excited to share this experience with her and just spend some good time alone with my little sis. But I had this HUGE thing that kept getting in the way of our good time. Everyday at around

3pm I would tell my sister that I needed a nap and would proceed to the cabin where I would order room service. Not only was I LYING to my sister, but I was literally stuffing my face in between meals, secretly I might add, on a cruise ship no less! My mind and heart were so out of control and unguarded that I would eat my room service as quickly as possible so that I could stash the tray down the hallway in front of another guest's door. Because I, OF COURSE, couldn't be caught eating in between meals. I spent the majority of the week sick and stuffed beyond full as I tried desperately to act normal in front of my sister.

It wasn't until last year that I reluctantly told my sister the truth as I shared the relief of finally being free from my eating disorder. She laughed out loud as she exclaimed, "I wondered why that cabin kept ordering trays and trays of food. I thought they must never be leaving their room. Maybe they were on their honeymoon or something…" The result for me of my heart being unguarded was that the rest of my life was unguarded. I ruined a wonderful vacation and missed spending time with my lovely sister because of my need to give in to my unruly heart.

Did you know that the Bible says that our hearts are wicked and will try to trick us? This is another verse used often in Christian circles yet is rarely—if ever—taught correctly.

> ### Jeremiah 17:9-10
> *9 "The heart is deceitful above all things*
> *and beyond cure.*
> *Who can understand it?*
> *10 "I the Lord search the heart*
> *and examine the mind,*

*to reward each person according to their conduct,*
*according to what their deeds deserve."*

ABOVE ALL THINGS...there is that wording again. Did
you catch it? According to this verse, our hearts are THE
MOST deceitful thing in our lives. I love the question this
verse puts forward: "Who can know it?" Honestly, when
I memorized this verse as a youth, I never thought twice
about the meaning of this verse. Yeah, I know I can't trust
my feelings. My heart is going to deceive me. But in the
real life messy situations, I trusted my heart anyway.

The next verse actually answers the question verse 9
asks. God KNOWS OUR HEARTS. He is the one that
searches and knows our hearts deeper than anyone else.
He understands the depths of our depravity and rewards
us according to our deeds, which are a direct result of our
wicked hearts. Do you see a pattern here yet?

### FIRST
...we must guard our hearts.
### SECOND
...everything we do in life comes from our hearts.
### THIRD
...our lives will reflect the condition of our hearts.
### FOURTH
...our hearts are wicked and in need of a cure.
### FIFTH
...God knows our hearts and expects us to look
after them.

The pattern we see in all of these verses about our heart is a
CALL TO ACTION. None of these verses says, "Let's just

leave our hearts alone and see what happens." They never once tell us, "If you give your heart free reign, then your life will turn out exactly the way you always dreamed." Those things sound suspiciously like the things the world tells us. "Always trust your heart...it will never mislead you." "Give in to your heart; it will be the best thing you can do for yourself!" "Always look out for number one and do the things that make YOU happy." The Biblical message of the heart is in direct opposition to the lies the world tells us, and yet we buy the world's lies. We believe that our happiness is the top priority in our lives, and we disregard the earth-shattering truth that in order to live our most fulfilled life, we MUST guard our heart...from ourselves. You and I are not trustworthy. Our hearts will lead us astray.

So where must we go for the real joy? We must go to God and carefully cultivate and guard our wayward hearts, against even ourselves.

> **Ephesians 4:17-24**
> "So I tell you this, and insist on it in the Lord, that you must no longer live as the Gentiles do, in the futility of their thinking. 18 They are darkened in their understanding and separated from the life of God because of the ignorance that is in them due to the hardening of their hearts. 19 Having lost all sensitivity, they have given themselves over to sensuality so as to indulge in every kind of impurity, and they are full of greed.
> 20 That, however, is not the way of life you learned 21 when you heard about Christ and were taught in him in accordance with the truth that is in

*Jesus. 22 You were taught, with regard to your former way of life, to put off your old self, which is being corrupted by its deceitful desires; 23 to be made new in the attitude of your minds; 24 and to put on the new self, created to be like God in true righteousness and holiness."*

These verses are RICH with truth about what our lives are meant to look like after Jesus saves us. He changes us; He convicts of sin. Most importantly, He gives us control over our minds, if we choose to grasp it. Verse 17 establishes that there are people who live their lives in futility of the mind. The exact definition of futility is pointlessness or uselessness. In other words, they go through life never having control of their minds in any way. As believers in Jesus, our call to action in this verse is clear. Do not live like those people. Why? Because they lack understanding and are separated from God. They are ignorant because their hearts haven't been cultivated properly. They lack every form of morality or sensitivity to the sins they wallow in. They are greedy and full of me-mindedness. Basically, they are the people of America, right now.

WOW, is that humbling to anyone else? Do you see yourself in that way? Do you find yourself drawn away easily into the things you should be avoiding? What about the shows we watch on TV? Or the music that pumps through every store in the US? The poisoning of our hearts and minds can happen so quickly; it seeps into our lives at every turn. We are drawn into the enticement of a life free of difficulty. If only we could live on a deserted island all by ourselves and have everything our heart desires. I can easily imagine myself sitting on a white sandy beach with a fruity drink and umbrella, with a tall handsome man fanning me while I bask in the beautiful sunlight. Or maybe a solo cruise where I don't need to cook or clean or think about anything outside of which area of the ship will be the quietest for reading my fifth book of the week.

Do you notice the call to action that comes in verses 20-24? They clearly lay out the life we have been called to as believers. First, we are not meant to live just like the people around us. Second, when we learned the truth of Jesus and believed, He showed us a way of escape from that inevitably empty life. We are called to put off the old person that we were that was corrupt and deceitful. And now we are made new in the ATTITUDE OF OUR MINDS. We now get to put on the new self and live like God in righteousness and holiness. What an amazing promise! Because of Jesus, we have the ability to change the attitude of our minds. According to Philippians 2, we literally get to have the same mind (or attitude) that Christ has because of His sacrifice for our sins. How freaking cool is that?

I have to admit, when I realized the mind and heart connection, it was overwhelming at first. How do I do that? How do I guard my heart and cultivate my mind so I am no longer drawn to the empty things of this world? How would I even start making this huge change in my life? Here is what I figured out: It is literally as simple as making the choice to be in control of the things I think about and believe.

## 2. BIBLICAL FOUNDATION FOR RENEWING YOUR MIND

We must renew our minds. Remember what RENEW actually means? It simply means to work hard at making something new. It is an ongoing process to restore what is broken or damaged. Our minds are definitely damaged and in need of serious repair.

The things we are bombarded with in our culture everyday stick with us. Whether or not we want to admit it, we are influenced by the lewd, unfiltered things our mind hears and sees daily. An example of this is TV shows and music that make foul language seem normal. Or that inner voice that tells you, "It is just one time; it will feel so good; nobody will know; have some fun." Or the gossip that happens at that one co-worker's desk in the office. Or how about our self-centered desire for our comfort above all else, including our families, God, and others?

The answer from God's Word is a simple command: "Renew your mind." Three little words, and yet it might as well be "learn to fly." We are as unlikely to renew our minds accidentally as we are to sprout wings and take flight. It is contrary to everything we are by nature. **Renewing our minds isn't just a single call to action once in a while. It is a daily, necessary part of the Christian life.** Without it, we get carried away into the easy-to-access ways of this world.

This Biblical concept can literally change the life you live today and will affect the rest of your life if you make it a simple daily practice.

***Romans 12:1,2***

*"Therefore, I urge you, brothers and sisters, in view
of God's mercy, to offer your bodies as a living
sacrifice, holy and pleasing to God—this is your true
and proper worship. 2 Do not conform to the pattern of
this world, but be transformed by the renewing of your
mind. Then you will be able to test and approve what
God's will is—his good, pleasing and perfect will."*

Paul urges us to give up ourselves, not because it is the
right thing to do, but simply because of God's mercy on
our lives. He calls us to live our lives as living sacrifices
to God because it is the only way to properly worship God.
Verse two continues with another two-part action for us
to take: First, do not conform. Second, be transformed by
the renewing of our minds. The reason? So that we know
what God's perfect will is for us. It goes without saying
that if we aren't renewing our minds, then we are unable to
test and approve what God's real will is for our life. How
are you doing with all of those commands? When you look
at it as a whole, it seems completely overwhelming, right?

But the breakdown of these verses is simple. Without
God, none of those things are possible for us. Each action
statement has a qualifying statement with it in this passage.
Did you notice?

**BECAUSE OF GOD'S MERCY ⇨ WE SHOULD BE
LIVING SACRIFICES**

**KNOWING GOD'S WILL FOR OUR LIVES ⇨ COMES
THROUGH THE RENEWAL OF OUR MINDS**

So, just in case you were confused, the mercy we have received from God is the free gift of salvation given to us through the shed blood of Jesus on the cross. I don't want to go past this point without first sharing with you the most important piece of this mind-renewal thing: a personal relationship with the God of the universe. Without understanding the Gospel first, it is impossible to grasp this concept fully. The principle of renewing our minds is predicated by the saving power of the Gospel in our lives and the indwelling of the Holy Spirit. Without those two components, the Gospel and the Holy Spirit, the rest of this message and book is utterly worthless.

# THE GOSPEL IN A NUTSHELL:

**WE ARE SINNERS. THE COST OF OUR SIN IS DEATH AND ETERNAL SEPARATION FROM A HOLY GOD.**

*Romans 3:23, James 1:15, Romans 5:12, 1 Corinthians 15:21*

**WE ARE ENEMIES OF GOD BECAUSE OF OUR SIN.**

*Romans 5:10a, Ephesians 2:3*

**IN SPITE OF OUR SIN, GOD MADE A WAY FOR US TO HAVE A RIGHT RELATIONSHIP WITH HIM.**

*Romans 5:10, Romans 5:8, Titus 3:3*

**JESUS, WHO WAS GOD IN THE FLESH, CAME TO THIS EARTH TO PAY THE PENALTY WE OWED FOR OUR SIN, WHICH WAS DEATH.**

*John 3:16, 1 Peter 2:24. John 1:1, 14*

**JESUS NOT ONLY PAID FOR OUR SIN, BUT ALSO GAVE TO US HIS RIGHTEOUSNESS.**

*2 Corinthians 5:21, 1 Peter 2:24, Romans 4:5, Romans 8:1*

**IF WE BELIEVE IN JESUS AND FULLY SURRENDER OUR LIVES TO HIM, THEN HE GIVES US THE FREE GIFT OF ETERNAL LIFE.**

*1 John 5:9-13, Romans 6:23, Romans 10:9,10, 1 John 1:9*

That's it...that's the Gospel in a nutshell. Isn't it beautiful? And so simple. Jesus gives us what we don't deserve and takes upon Himself the punishment that we do deserve. It is a simple exchange, and yet it was the costliest exchange in the history of this world.

Even if you are already a true believer in Jesus and have placed your faith in Him, it is still important to preach this message to yourself often.

***You must understand the Gospel before the principles taught in this book can become lasting change in your life.*** Not only did Jesus give us His perfect righteousness, He also gave us the gift of the Holy Spirit. Through the power of the Holy Spirit, we are able to walk in a manner worthy of God like Romans 12 says. Because of the Holy Spirit, we (for the first time) have the ability to go contrary to our human nature (as sinners) and become the new self as described in Ephesians chapter 4.

> *Galatians 5:1*
> *"It is for freedom that Christ has set us free. Stand firm, then, and do not let yourselves be burdened again by a yoke of slavery."* Slaves to sin

Did you see that very important truth? Read it again one more time...slowly...just the first part. We were set free from the slavery of sin and death so that...we could be free! TA-DA! Do you get it? Before Jesus set us free, we were slaves to our natural desires. We were slaves to the death that had a hold on us. We couldn't break free; we had no ability to go contrary to our nature as sinful human beings.

AND NOW we have the ability to CHOOSE freedom because, not only did Jesus set us free, He also GAVE US FREEDOM. Let me put it this way. When Jesus paid the price for our sins and gave us life, He also woke us up so that we were able to choose freedom (the new self) every day. For the first time in our lives we could make choices contrary to our human nature. We are free.

And that's what renewing our minds is; *it is us choosing things contrary to our human nature. It is throwing away our old self and being renewed day-by-day.*
Amazing, isn't it?

One of the coolest parts about understanding the importance of renewing our minds is understanding that we are not meant to do it alone. It doesn't come from our own power. We have the Holy Spirit to walk alongside us. He gives us the power to be able to choose life and freedom every day.

> **Galatians 5:16-17**
> *"So I say, walk by the Spirit, and you will not gratify the desires of the flesh. 17 For the flesh desires what is contrary to the Spirit, and the Spirit what is contrary to the flesh. They are in conflict with each other, so that you are not to do whatever you want. "*

The Holy Spirit is a partner with us in the call to renew our minds. He isn't our conscience that makes us feel guilty. He is literally a companion that walks through each day with us. If we walk by the Spirit, then we will not walk by the flesh. Simply put, He makes the process of renewing our minds and laying down our desires as a living sacrifice

43

possible and painless. It is not in our power that we do it. It is only the power of the Holy Spirit living in us that makes it possible.

You will start to recognize those times in your life when you begin relying on your own power to renew your mind. It is painful! You will become self-focused and obsessed with not messing up (perfection lie again). You will become stressed out over the smallest temptation and will find yourself giving in to your me-mindedness more often. That's because renewing your mind isn't meant to be done on your own. The Holy Spirit is a willing participant in the renewal process if you allow Him to be.

The Holy Spirit is actually a participant in this process even when we don't want Him to be, and that's when the renewal gets really painful. The Bible tells us that God desires our growth and maturity as we walk in our faith. When we don't listen, the Bible says that God chastises us like a father does his child. The renewal will happen either way, but you get to make a choice. Will you willfully and joyfully renew your mind with the Holy Spirit as your close companion? Or will God have to show you the hard way that renewal must happen in your life? You get to decide.

***Choose wisely.***

## 3. BIBLICAL FOUNDATION FOR MEDITATION

Now please don't close this book right now because Britney is getting into that weird hybrid Christianity/ Eastern religion thing. Bear with me for just one moment. The first thing I want to throw out there is this: Eastern

meditation practices are 100% different from Biblical meditation, although some of the principles are similar. I will never ask you to empty yourself of all your thoughts in order to connect with the spirit of the universe. I will never ask you to sit in the butterfly position with your hands on your knees making the "OM" sound. That is not Godly or biblical meditation.

The point of biblical meditation is to refocus our minds on God and His Word. That's it.

The writer of Psalms often talks about the importance of meditating on God's Word. Did you know that prayer is actually a form of biblical meditation? The basic premise behind meditation in general is to calm the things around you (and in your mind) to focus on truth. The Bible even talks about meditating through music, one of my favorites.

What I want you to do right now is forget everything you ever thought you knew about meditation. Forget that yoga class you took once where you took 3 minutes to clear the space around you of negativity. We aren't talking about cleaning our chakras or allowing the universe to speak truth into us. Let's focus on what God's Word has to say about meditation because, let's face it, God's Word is the only opinion that matters here.

> ### Isaiah 26:3
> *"You will keep in perfect peace*
> *those whose minds are steadfast,*
> *because they trust in you."*

**Joshua 1:8**
*"Keep this Book of the Law always on your lips;
meditate on it day and night, so that you may be
careful to do everything written in it. Then you will be
prosperous and successful.*

**Psalm 1:2**
*"but his delight is in the law of the LORD, and on his
law he meditates day and night."*

**Psalm 19:14**
*"May these words of my mouth and this meditation of
my heart be pleasing in your sight, LORD, my Rock
and my Redeemer."*

**Psalm 119:15**
*"I meditate on your precepts and consider your ways."*

**Psalm 1:1-3**
*"Blessed is the one who does not walk in step with
the wicked or stand in the way that sinners take or sit
in the company of mockers, 2 but whose delight is in
the law of the LORD, and who meditates on his law
day and night. 3 That person is like a tree planted
by streams of water, which yields its fruit in season
and whose leaf does not wither— whatever they do
prospers."*

The Bible mentions meditation 23 times, not including the
times the concepts of meditation are taught, and it is always
in context of looking to God, His Word, and His goodness.
At every retreat I lead, I have one night of prayer, worship,

and meditation. It is a time for the women to just sit quietly with God and leave their stresses and anxieties in the lap of Jesus. There is no talking, just silent prayer and times of silence to sit with God. It always starts out awkwardly and slowly, but by the end of the hour there is a noticeable difference in the women and they don't want to stop. They seem lighter, their minds are free of stress, and they are always amazed at how God communicated with them in their silence.

As I talk about meditation later in this book in connection with renewing your mind, give it a chance. I will never ask you to do anything contrary to God's Word, and I have a feeling it will become one of your favorite times with God.

Romans 8:26 says that in those times when we don't have words to utter, the Holy Spirit speaks on our behalf. But honestly, as women when is the last time we even let there be silence in our time with God? This is something that I have to consciously do in my quiet time. In the past, my time with God included reading my Bible and then talking AT God for several minutes during my prayer time. After that I felt alright about checking off my "Good Christian" checkbox for the day. Until a few years ago, I never stopped to allow the Holy Spirit of God to commune with me in my soul, as I sat in silence. Now it's one of the sweetest times I have with God.

**How about you? Could you benefit from a practice of daily mind renewal and meditation, if it would bring about that soul rest that you need?**

# CHAPTER THREE

# YOUR AMAZING BRAIN

When I was a young child, I became convinced of a great many things that were untrue.

One thing that specifically stands out is my belief that I was pronouncing and spelling words correctly when, in fact, I was sadly mistaken. Britney as a 6-year-old was quite confident when it came to her spelling. One day in first grade I became so upset over my 90% score on a spelling test, I cried the entire school day until my parents were called to pick me up. I went home so upset at my teacher for marking my test score wrong. My parents couldn't console me.

This lasted for an entire week until my teacher asked me to look up a word in the classroom dictionary one day. I had a brilliant idea! I was going to prove my teacher wrong. After I looked up the word my teacher assigned, I secretly looked up the two spelling words she had marked wrong on my test. I was so convinced that I was right that, when I couldn't find the words spelled correctly (my 6-year-old spelling), I believed they had been left out of the dictionary. I mentioned to my teacher that those words I missed on the test weren't even in the dictionary. She smiled at me as she proceeded to look up the CORRECT spelling of words in the dictionary to set my wayward mind right. As I got older, that desire to prove I was right took many, many years to break.

I tell this story to illustrate the power of thought and our ability to believe things that are simply not true. We can also believe things that are harmful to us. A more recent example came from my eating disorder. As a teenager, I became convinced that, because I was curvier than my classmates, I was fat and needed to lose weight. As I entered college, I was surrounded by college girls who wore smaller sized clothes than I did, and I felt like a huge whale. So I began dieting...ALL THE TIME. During my first year of college, I got down to my lowest weight since middle school by skipping breakfast, eating a small lunch, and most of the time skipping dinner as well. It was during this time that my first binging episode happened, and I was mortified. It only got worse from that point on. I dieted for 3 weeks without a binge incident, and then all of a sudden—BOOM—it happened again. The binges became more and more frequent until I lived in constant terror of when it would happen again. That behavior pattern of starving myself and binging came from one simple, harmful thought: "I am bigger than my classmates." I know I am not alone in those thoughts because our culture obsesses over our bodies at every turn. **That feeling of inadequacy, or not measuring up, is a harmful one that must be addressed or it will quickly take over our minds.** So let's address it!

Have you ever stopped to consider your brain and the power of your own thoughts? Your brain sits in your skull and makes your entire body do what it is supposed to do—and sometimes what it's not supposed to do. It literally controls our entire lives, and yet most of us never stop to consider the power of the brain.

One thing that is interesting to note as we get started in this chapter is the connection between the brain and heart. We talked about this a little bit in the last chapter. God's Word uses the "mind" and "heart" interchangeably to mean the essence of a human being or our personality. While our hearts actually have very little to do with our emotions and decision-making processes, we talk about our hearts much more often than our brains.

This chapter is probably the most fascinating to me and took me the longest to write. We are going to dig deep into the science behind our thought life and why it's important to understand how our brains function. Other authors, like Brene Brown, who study neuroscience are the authorities on this subject. I am in no way an expert on neuroscience, but I have spent much time studying and figuring out the brain's functionality. Thank goodness for people who have a desire to share their knowledge with the world!

**Renewing your mind is an intentional act of mindfulness.** If that word mindfulness scares you, then you are not alone. As I said earlier, when I first started practicing mindfulness, I tried to hide what I was learning from those in my world. I didn't want anyone to think I was a heretic or getting into that "new age" stuff. However, as I went further in my studies, I kept getting drawn back to God's Word and the brain and heart connection found in scripture. And you know what I realized? God CREATED OUR BRAINS TO WORK THE WAY THEY DO. It's not "new age-y" to consider the function of our brains and renewing our minds. That concept goes back to creation when God created man to think, make decisions, and have emotions. It's older than Eastern religions and their religious meditation practices. **The human brain and its functionality is literally God's design on display.** Isn't that a cool thought?

While we are going to focus on the science behind the way our brains work, we are going to do it through the lens of the Master Creator. He created each individual neuron in our brains and made each to function in a very specific way. Our brains are an amazing masterpiece of the Almighty God. I think this process will give you a deeper love and appreciation for the God who created and designed our brains so intricately and lovingly.

For just a moment, think through the modern marvels of 21st century technology. When I was in 6th grade, I remember a video that my science teacher played for us as an example of some new up-and-coming technology: a video phone that, for only $.45 cents a minute, could call someone across the ocean who happened to have the same model phone you did. (All for the low price of only 3 payments of $199.) I sat in awe of that video phone that day and remember thinking, "That would be amazing, but it will probably never happen." Little did I know, less than 15 years later, I would be carrying that technology with me everywhere I go. I would bet you even have a miniature computer nearby called a cell phone. Am I right?

The technological advances being made today are so far beyond where we were even 20 years ago that it's astounding. Now I don't know about you, but if it were up to me, all human beings would be living in hovels and scavenging for food. Luckily, it's not up to me, and God gave other people the ability to think outside of the technological box. In God's intricate design, He gave people individual talents, knowledge, and skills. He gave us the ability to learn and grow in our understanding. He created our brains as the most flawless and intricate computer system of all time. Yet the huge technological advances we are seeing in our world today pale in comparison to the human brain. The comparison between a modern computer system and our brains is a really cool thing to look at when we are trying to understand our brain functionality better.

A computer's functionality and operating system is found in a place called the motherboard and is the place where every computer function begins. Contained within that motherboard are the hard drives and memory that store information. The operating system tells the computer what types of things it should do and the way to display information. When it malfunctions or gets a virus, there is antivirus software to protect the system from totally failing. When a computer works properly, it is one of the most useful inventions of all time. But when it malfunctions... well, I don't think I need to tell you...there are words and frustrations. Right?

Our brains, while much more intricate, are like our computer system's motherboard. Each piece of our brain functions with a specific purpose; and when it malfunctions or "overheats," it can get messy. I believe the Bible talks about our minds and hearts so often because God knows the importance of a good maintenance plan. That sounds like a funny thought, but think about it. Every single action we take in our life comes from a brain function. We literally can do nothing without both our brain and our heart functioning. Once the brain and heart stop functioning, we are dead. God gave us instructions about maintaining our thought life and hearts/minds. It's the process of renewing our minds and meditating on God's Word.

## THE LIMBIC SYSTEM AND AMYGDALA

Let's take some time right now to dive into the science
of your brain. From the time you are born, there is a part
of your brain that functions at 100% all the time. It's the
emotional center of your brain, or as the experts call it,
the amygdala, which is housed in the limbic system. The
amygdala is involved in the processing of your emotions,
especially anger and fear. The experts call it your survival
brain or lizard brain, and it is the one area of your brain that
is fully formed at birth. It's the part of your brain that tells
a child to scream when they are startled or cry when they
are afraid. It's also your fight or flight instinct and warns
you of impending danger. While it is very useful, it has
the ability to throw your entire system out of whack when
allowed to have more control that it should have.

When your amygdala is damaged and operating outside
of its normal function—or not functioning at all—then all
kinds of crazy things can happen. Many studies conclude
that the amygdala is the thing that has kept humans alive
and avoiding dangerous situations throughout history.
When your amygdala is damaged, you no longer can sense
danger, and the fight or flight instinct is completely gone, or
at the very least, severely hampered. You are more likely
to take big risks in life, even when that risk has no potential
benefit to you.

## THE PREFRONTAL CORTEX

The prefrontal cortex is at the heart of who you are as
a person. It's often called the personality center, and it

controls all of the information you experience through your senses. It's the part of your brain that makes the majority of the logical and daily decisions for your life. I like to call it the logical brain, because it literally is created to control the executive function of your body including sight, sound, taste, touch, and speech. It is the part of the brain that allows you to plan for the future and make wise decisions outside of the moment. It has the ability to see far beyond the now and decide the best path to take each day to end up in the right place down the road. It controls and adjusts your thoughts and daily actions. But the one downside to the prefrontal cortex is that it grows and learns with us. The prefrontal cortex isn't fully formed until a person is around 24 years old. That can be a problem.

This means from birth we are emotional creatures; and since the amygdala is firing on all cylinders, it trains the prefrontal cortex to respond in a certain way to its constant communication and nagging. Though the prefrontal cortex is the one that makes final decisions, it's a big proponent of listening to the amygdala. You could say the amygdala is somewhat like the older, hormonal, and emotional, teenage sister.

Take a moment to think about a 2-year old in your life. They are beginning to have more coordination and starting to talk. They are learning hand-eye coordination and can understand most words spoken to them, but their language and speech skills are nowhere near perfected. Their natural response is still one born out of pure, raw emotion. If they see something they want, it's MINE! If they are afraid, they cry; if they are angry, they cry; if they are tired, they cry. In fact, even kids who have had good parenting and discipline will still react emotionally and cry for many years into childhood until that option is no longer beneficial as a means of getting what they want or need.

Because a child's amygdala is running on all cylinders, they lack the ability to think beyond the moment they are currently living in. By the age of 3-4, they are beginning to learn the importance of delayed gratification, but it's still a foreign concept that needs daily reminding by loving parenting.

This means, from the time we are children, we are taught to form our logical thought patterns by our parents, teachers, and other influences in our lives. It's also why education is so much easier when children are young because their brains are literally learning and growing with them. I'm telling you, God understood what He was doing when He created our brains to function the way they do. It makes the verse in Proverbs take on greater meaning.

*Proverbs 22:6*
*"Start children off on the way they should go, and even when they are old they will not turn from it."*

As a culture, this Biblical concept is being increasingly lost. We are being taught that a child's identity is something that they need to develop and work through on their own. Young parents are being looked down upon for their strict guidance and discipline. Children are raising themselves in America, and it's becoming more and more apparent that it's not working. Proverbs 22:6 is wisdom straight from God. If you train children in the ways of God, teach morality, love, thankfulness, God-mindedness, hard work, etc., that is who they will become. It goes without saying that these formative years of their lives are the ones they need the most guidance in. The Bible never says to be best friends with your child. It never says that a child's gratification and happiness are the parents' only responsibility. What the Bible does teach is the exact opposite. Children are to honor their parents; parents are meant to love their children, and a part of that love is sometimes hard love and discipline.

## THE RETICULAR ACTIVATING SYSTEM/ NEUROPLASTICITY

As human beings, we are HIGHLY impressionable in the formative years (birth to 24) because of our growing brains and limited brain functionality. We believe things that aren't true all the time, and our brains store those untruths away in long term storage for later. Our brains have the most high-tech filtering system ever created called the Reticular Activating System (RAS). We will talk a lot more about it in the next chapter, but I want to mention it here because of its importance when understanding our brains. The RAS can filter millions of pieces of information in a single second, but it only allows the important things to be seen in our conscious mind. The RAS is filtering out unimportant information and bringing to light important information every second of every day. Scientists call these two different filters our conscious brain and subconscious brain.

The RAS is so good at its job that it works with the rest of the brain to create pathways called neural pathways. Neural pathways are shortcuts in our brain that get us to our logical conclusion faster. Each of us has our own highly personalized neural pathways, and these are formed by patterns of habit in our lives. Have I lost you yet? I hope not, because we are just getting to the good stuff!

The scientific term for the forming of new pathways in our brain is called neuroplasticity. Neuroplasticity is the brain's ability to create shortcuts between the brain synapse (electrical or chemical signals passed between brain cells) so that we react and function a certain way in situations. Factors such as our upbringing, moral character, religion, political leaning, and parents determine the things our brains define as important or not. While neuroplasticity is something that happens throughout our lifetime, our brains create and prune out unused neural pathways all the time.

A good example of this is that 2-year-old we were talking about earlier. As he learns and grows and realizes that crying is not a great way to communicate logically through an interaction with another human being, that behavior slowly gets pruned from his brain. It is replaced with the ability to speak using words and much less emotion. How your brain decides which connections to prune out depends on your life experiences and how recently connections have been used. In general, neuroplasticity is a way for your brain to fine-tune itself for efficiency. It tends to keep doing the things you have always done and avoid change at all costs.

As we get further into the concepts of renewing your mind, we are going to talk a lot about change and the brain's emotional response to it. If you take the concepts in this book and put them into practice, you are going to start seeing emotional flags begin to pop up. While our brains are conditioned for normal change and growth, it's not something that our brains particularly like or enjoy. **Change is uncomfortable and new and contrary to our engrained neural pathways.** Keep that in mind as we continue.

## CONSCIOUS AND SUBCONSCIOUS THOUGHT

Conscious and subconscious thought is also important to understand in order to renew our minds. As we just said, you are thinking about and processing through thousands of pieces of information at a time. In recent years, studies in neurology have shown that as an adult about 95% of our daily activities happen in our subconscious thought, which means that only 5% of the decisions our brain makes on a daily basis are conscious decisions.

I find this piece of information fascinating. Each morning when I wake up, I climb out of bed and place my feet on the floor; I walk across the hall to my bathroom, where I go to the bathroom and brush my teeth. At this point I normally head down to my comfy chair for a quiet time in my Bible and some coffee. When I get hungry, I make some breakfast and start my work day. Those are the conscious choices I make every morning; but in between all of those conscious decisions, my brain is making all kinds of tiny unconscious decisions as well. What if, when I got out of bed, my brain didn't tell my legs to support my weight? What if reading my Bible was like it used to be in kindergarten when I had to struggle through every word as I sounded out the consonants and vowels? What if my hand refused to hold my toothbrush up to my teeth? Are you thankful for your subconscious mind yet? I know I sure am.

Most of the time, this isn't a problem. I mean, how exhausting would it be to consciously think through each finger grabbing our toothbrush, keeping our muscles tight so we don't drop it, and making the right circular motions, and moving in time to reach every single tooth, while also remembering to stand upright? Phew…exhausting.

But that subconscious mind is also the thing that automates our thought life, including our emotions, actions, and reactions. It teaches our minds to react a certain way to circumstances based on our past or learned behaviors. It communicates thoroughly about our habits, past hurts, and individuality so that what is normal for us continues to be normal.

The brain's automating and running of our lives becomes a problem when we cultivate and create bad habits in our lives. Remember college when we stayed up until 2am with friends only to get up at 6:30am to make it in time for our 7am class? Oh, and we procrastinate that 22-page paper until the week before it's due. (Still one of the worst decisions I ever made…the 7AM class, I mean.) We teach our brains to procrastinate, lust, be angry, hold grudges, not trust people, and look to other people for approval instead of looking to God. We have taught our brains to run to things that are not healthy for us but have become habits in our lives. This is why I think the Bible has to keep reminding us to renew our minds. Renewing our minds is an act of intentional change and revision. It's using our conscious mind rather than allowing the subconscious to keep running amok in our lives on autopilot.

In the next couple of chapters, we are going to learn exactly HOW to renew our mind effectively, but I want to spend the rest of this chapter focusing on our brain functionality and looking at what God's Word says about God's good creation, our mind.

As human beings we have something inside of us that no other creature on the face of the planet has. The Bible says that God created us to commune within ourselves, and that we were created in His image. We know from the Bible that God is a being who is 3-in-1, the Father, the Son and the Holy Spirit. Although our minds cannot fully grasp an infinite Creator who is 3-in-1, we believe it, because we know God's Word is trustworthy and infallible. Human beings were created in the image of God with a body, a soul and a spirit, three different parts of us that all make up who we are. Although I am not sure what each one of those parts entails specifically, I do know they allow us to reason and think things through unlike any other creature on this earth. I would like to point out what I am **not** saying right now. I am not saying that our body, mind, and soul are a perfect replica of God's triune nature. It's simply an easy way for us to grasp the concept.

### Genesis 1:26-28
*"Then God said, "Let us make mankind in our image, in our likeness, so that they may rule over the fish in the sea and the birds in the sky, over the livestock and all the wild animals, and over all the*

*creatures that move along the ground."*
*27 So God created mankind in his own image,*
 *in the image of God he created them;*
 *male and female he created them.*
*28 God blessed them and said to them, "Be fruitful and*
*increase in number; fill the earth and subdue it. Rule*
*over the fish in the sea and the birds in the sky and*
*over every living creature that moves on the ground."*

Let me paint a picture for you. I grew up on a 6-acre farm
in the middle of Utah where we raised horses, cows, pigs,
and goats, and we had cats and a dog. I learned early that
animals were hard work! But one of my favorite things to
do was sit on the fence next to the cow pasture or the pig
pen. Animals are so fascinating and yet so predictable.
Each day they did the exact same thing and never wavered.
When my dad brought them food, they'd eat, then lay back
down or graze or play with each other. In all my years
of sitting on that fence, I never saw them do anything
particularly surprising or amazing. They were simply
content to exist in the place they had always existed.

On our farm, we always had cows raised specifically for
meat. My dad would never let us name the cows anything
other than what they would eventually become. We had
cows named Hamburger, Steak, and Meatloaf. We even
once had pigs named Bacon and Pork Chop. Morbid, I
know, but I have to admit it definitely did the trick. We
never once got overly attached to our meal-named animals.
One of our chores occasionally was to feed the cows
or horses and help my dad fill their water tanks. Every
morning, to feed them, Dad would unlatch the gate and
walk into the pasture, then re-latch the gate as we left. The

cows would stand there and watch him undo the latch on the gate EVERY MORNING; but as long as my dad kept the fence maintained, those cows never figured out how to get out of that field, and to my knowledge they didn't even try to escape. Now what if I put you in that field? How long would it take you to escape the confines of that fence and gate? About as long as it takes to walk up to the gate, unlatch it, and walk out, right? Or you might simply climb over the fence if the gate was locked.

Now imagine in your mind a maximum security prison. There are guard towers with high walls and barbed wire, and at every post there is an armed guard. Inside the prison blocks, not only are you behind your locked prison cell door, but the cell block door and the outer door. All these doors are accessible only from the outside by an armed prison guard. Yet no matter how many checkpoints and security features they put into a prison, men will figure out how to escape. Every time I picture this in my mind, I immediately think of a popular TV show a few years ago called "Prison Break." It didn't matter how many prisons the main character was in, or what safeguards they set up, he was always able to find a way to escape.

Now imagine with me for a moment that we put a cow into that prison cell. How long do you think it would take a cow to escape a maximum security prison? That cow would stand in that prison cell eating, sleeping, and chewing its cud until the day it dies. **Human beings are different from animals. We were created with the ability to reason and think on our own by the grand design of a good God and Master Creator.**

### Genesis 2:15-22

*"The Lord God took the man and put him in the
Garden of Eden to work it and take care of it. 16 And
the Lord God commanded the man, "You are free to
eat from any tree in the garden; 17 but you must not
eat from the tree of the knowledge of good and evil, for
when you eat from it you will certainly die."
18 The Lord God said, "It is not good for the man to
be alone. I will make a helper suitable for him."
19 Now the Lord God had formed out of the ground
all the wild animals and all the birds in the sky. He
brought them to the man to see what he would name
them; and whatever the man called each living
creature, that was its name. 20 So the man gave
names to all the livestock, the birds in the sky and
all the wild animals.
But for Adam no suitable helper was found.
21 So the Lord God caused the man to fall into a
deep sleep; and while he was sleeping, he took one
of the man's ribs and then closed up the place with
flesh. 22 Then the Lord God made a woman from the
rib[h] he had taken out of the man, and he brought her
to the man."*

This passage of scripture is so cool because not only does
God make Adam the caretaker of the entire earth's creation,
we also see God creating Eve. I love the wording of this
passage in the original Hebrew. The words "suitable
helper" in this passage mean so much more than it says
in English. This title, "suitable helper," is the title God so
lovingly gave to all women, not just Eve. In the original
Hebrew, we see the concept of Eve being the perfect
"companion" to Adam. Eve was not created above or

below Adam; she was complementary to him. She had the ability to be everything he was not. The word for "helper" here is the Hebrew word "ezer" which is a title that is also used of God throughout the Bible. It speaks to the innate nature of the "ezer," or helper, to perfectly fit the needed situation. In other words, God created women unique and distinct from **men so that they could affect change in ways a man can't. There is no question that women's brains function ver**y differently than men's. Women tend to feel more deeply and are generally much more in tune with the emotional responses of people.

I am saying all of these things to show you the power of our brains and God's purpose behind its complex features. We were CREATED to think and reason and invent and grow and change. Our intricately designed brains allow people to engineer amazing buildings that will stand for hundreds and sometimes thousands of years. There is no other creature on the planet that has the ability to reason within their own minds and create things like human beings can.

**That's why it is so important that we USE the brains God has given us to have the life that we were created to live.** We have this fantastic tool inside our heads that gives us the ability to make wise decisions and huge life changes if we are only able to override our normal thought processes.

Let's use our brains the way they were created to work.

# CHAPTER FOUR

# CULTIVATE
# THANKFULNESS

A few years ago, as I was going through the worst of my eating disorder, I fell into a deep depression. It got so bad at times that I would literally stay in bed all day to avoid a binge. I figured if I stayed in bed, then I wouldn't be eating. The difficulty came when I finally did have to get out of bed, and the kitchen would come into view. It sounds ridiculous to be saying this out loud now, but at the time it was a very real and awful struggle I faced. The worst part was that, even when I was avoiding food by staying in bed, my mind constantly thought about what I would eat next and how much food I could eat.

During this time in my life, I hated who I was and what my eating disorder had made me. I thought, like so many Christian people do, that there was something wrong with my walk with God, because the fruit of the spirit is self-control, and that is one thing I KNEW I definitely did not have. Yes, I was self-controlled in most other areas of my life, but when it came to food, I was a loose cannon. I lived in a constant state of panic, never knowing when the next binging episode would come. And the more I tried to control my eating disorder, the worse the problem got.

After years of this being my norm, it began to become my identity. I was the girl who was obsessed with food. I knew the best restaurants, the best thing on the menu, and the thing that each restaurant was known for. In a world where being a "foodie" is becoming increasingly popular, I identified as the quintessential foodie at every turn. Others started to identify me that way as well. If someone needed a food recommendation, they would come to me. I was proud and disgusted with myself at the same time. The thing that I hated most about myself I also loved.

The thing I touted as my biggest strength had become my undoing.

I cannot tell you how many vacations I ruined because of my obsession with food. Instead of enjoying time with family and friends, I would spend every waking hour figuring out where our next meal would be and what I would order. If a person suggested we just stop along the road somewhere, I would have terrible anxiety until I was able to look up a possible restaurant in the vicinity that might be good. Forget spontaneity! When it came to food, I needed to be in control. What's funny is that my lack of control with food led to my need for control over which foods I put into my mouth. Those who know me now no longer see me that way. The person I am now is drastically different from that frantic, anxiety-ridden, miserable control freak, but I can't escape the fact that I was that person for a good portion of my life.

As I spoke to my aunt on the phone a few nights ago, she reminded me of a great truth. There is a big difference between guilt and shame. Guilt is feeling negative about something I HAVE DONE. Shame is feeling negative about who I AM. Shame is what I felt in my life for so many years, and sadly I don't believe I am alone in that. Shame affects our identity and becomes something that defines our lives. But it doesn't have to.

I look back on those years of my life now and I see such sadness and waste, but I also see great joy and growth that came from it. I see the mess of who I was now redeemed by the goodness of God. I see a false identity being torn down by the truth of who I am in Christ. I see how God used that horrible time to make me into an instrument that He could use for His glory. I see hopelessness and sorrow turned to joy and peace. I see God being glorified in His strength through my weakness, and I thank Him for it. But I can tell you right now that this view of myself did not come easily.

One of the most important tools we have when it comes to renewing our minds is gratitude. I would venture to say gratitude and thankfulness have the ability to change the outcome of ANY day. As we are on this journey of learning what it means to live a God-focused life instead of a Me-focused one, the first step is to give thanks. This is where we start. ─

The reason we start here is because thankfulness has a way of changing any situation or attitude. My practice (especially on days when I wake up on the wrong side of the bed) is to spend enough time being thankful that I can't help but smile. I have a thankfulness list written down so that on the days when I have a hard time finding things I am thankful for, it can help me get started. I cannot tell you how many days I started giving thanks, and when I went to bed at night my mind was still coming up with things I was grateful for.

The scientific reasoning behind a thankfulness practice is fascinating. Remember that little baby-carrot-shaped part of our brains called the reticular activating system that is our brain's filter? As a reminder, it is the mechanism God put in place so our brains wouldn't overload from the sheer amount of information the human brain processes at any given time. Scientists believe that at any second our brains are processing millions of pieces of information, but we are only consciously aware of about 50 things at any one moment.

Let's do an experiment. Wherever you are, stop what you are doing and focus on your surroundings. Right now I am sitting in a little tiny coffee shop and bakery in Preston, Idaho. There are at least three conversations going on around me, the radio is playing "Strawberry Wine", the drink cooler is running loudly, there is a child crying, cars are driving by on Main Street, my keyboard keys are clicking in time with my typing, and my coffee is cold. Those are the things I am currently aware of, but I couldn't tell you what the table next to me is talking about even though they are talking rather loudly...oh wait, they are talking about cars and specifically engine blocks. Did you notice what just happened there? Because I said I didn't know what those men were talking about, my brain corrected that thought by allowing me to hear their conversation for a moment. That's all because of this piece of our brain called the reticular activating system (RAS).

It is such a cool part of our brains that it may just be my favorite part, and as you saw from the last chapter, I am a freak when it comes to learning about the brain's functionality and how God's masterful creation works. The RAS is trained to pick up things that are important to us and are necessary for our survival. It is also trained to filter out the things that are not important to us. Have you ever wondered why individual political and life choices vary so much? Factors such as upbringing, race, class, and morality are huge factors. How can one person be completely convinced of the existence of a loving God and another person be convinced there is no God? Why do believers see the existence of God all around us when others don't? The answer is simpler than we might imagine.

Each person's RAS has been trained to see those things through careful cultivation. A great example of this in action is your first name. I bet if you were in a crowded room full of people with loud music playing in the background and someone yelled your name, you would hear it. Why? Because it is literally the first thing that our brain was trained to hear. In the same way, we can train our brains to search for gratitude and thankfulness.

Basically, what happens when we tell our brains to start searching for something (like gratitude), the reticular activating system is designed to continue to find evidence to support whatever we are searching for. So in the morning when we wake up, if the first thing we tell our brains to search for is thankfulness, then the rest of our day goes better because our brain finds new evidence and new thankfulness throughout our day. It's like going shopping for a new car, or more specifically a cherry red Chevy Mustang. As we begin the search, we may see a cherry red Chevy Mustang every once in a while, but the longer we search for it, the more we see them. It's not because the number of cherry red Chevy Mustang's on the road has increased in number, it's because now our brain is aware of them and constantly looking for them.

In the same way, **gratitude as a discipline and practice has a way of creating or multiplying gratefulness in our lives.** Even in the middle of difficult circumstances, our minds will continue to look for evidence of the things we are most grateful for as we cultivate this practice. It's surprising how often God's Word brings up the concept of gratitude, often manifested in a story that has very little to do with thankfulness.

### *Philippians 4:6-7*
*"Do not be anxious about anything, but in everything by prayer and supplication with thanksgiving let your requests be made known to God. And the peace of God, which surpasses all understanding, will guard your hearts and your minds in Christ Jesus."*

### *1 Thessalonians 5:16-18* says it best
*"Rejoice always, pray continually, give thanks in all circumstances; for this is God's will for you in Christ Jesus."*

Did you catch that last part? Thankfulness is God's will for us. Why? Why are these things (rejoicing, praying, thankfulness) so important to God? I think a simple answer lies in the example of the children of Israel. Although they had been delivered from slavery, they had to be reminded over and over again of God's goodness and provision in their lives.

Just like the children of Israel, we have a tendency to forget. We forget how much we loved our job when we started. We forget what it's like to live with "little to nothing" because we have been comfortable far too long. We forget that we are loved by God, we forget what it was like to be young, and we forget that some of the most difficult situations are temporary. **By practicing being**

**thankful, we are reminded of all of the good things in our lives and in turn reminded of God's graciousness in our lives.** We remember God's provision in that difficult situation when we were a young 20-something on the brink of being homeless. As believers, being thankful reminds us that no matter what is happening in our lives circumstantially, it pales in comparison to the riches of God's grace on our lives.

**Deuteronomy 8** is a great passage reminding us of the importance of gratitude and recounting all God has done for us. This was a speech Moses gave to the children of Israel about remembering God's goodness and their utter helplessness before they were to enter the land God had promised to them over 40 years earlier. Moses' plea was for the children of Israel to remember how God was their provider, to remember that nothing that they had or would possess comes outside of God's gracious provision.

*Be careful to follow every command I am giving you today, so that you may live and increase and may enter and possess the land the Lord promised on oath to your ancestors. 2 Remember how the Lord your God led you all the way in the wilderness these forty years, to humble and test you in order to know what was in your heart, whether or not you would keep his commands. 3 He humbled you, causing you to hunger and then feeding you with manna, which neither you nor your ancestors had known, to teach you that man does not live on bread alone but on every word that comes from the mouth of the Lord. 4 Your clothes did not wear out and your feet did not swell during these forty years. 5 Know*

then in your heart that as a man disciplines his son, so
the Lord your God disciplines you.

6 Observe the commands of the Lord your God,
walking in obedience to him and revering him. 7 For
the Lord your God is bringing you into a good land—a
land with brooks, streams, and deep springs gushing
out into the valleys and hills; 8 a land with wheat and
barley, vines and fig trees, pomegranates, olive oil and
honey; 9 a land where bread will not be scarce and you
will lack nothing; a land where the rocks are iron and
you can dig copper out of the hills.

10 When you have eaten and are satisfied, praise
the Lord your God for the good land he has given
you. 11 _Be careful that you do not forget the Lord your
God_, failing to observe his commands, his laws and his
decrees that I am giving you this day. 12 Otherwise,
when you eat and are satisfied, when you build fine
houses and settle down, 13 and when your herds and
flocks grow large and your silver and gold increase
and all you have is multiplied, 14 then your heart
will become proud and you will forget the Lord your
God, who brought you out of Egypt, out of the land of
slavery. 15 He led you through the vast and dreadful
wilderness, that thirsty and waterless land, with its
venomous snakes and scorpions. He brought you
water out of hard rock. 16 He gave you manna to
eat in the wilderness, something your ancestors had
never known, to humble and test you so that in the
end it might go well with you. 17 You may say to
yourself, "My power and the strength of my hands have
produced this wealth for me." 18 _But remember
the Lord your God_, for it is he who gives you the ability

*to produce wealth, and so confirms his covenant, which*
*he swore to your ancestors, as it is today.*
*19 If you ever forget the Lord your God and follow*
*other Gods and worship and bow down to them,*
*I testify against you today that you will surely be*
*destroyed. 20 Like the nations the Lord destroyed*
*before you, so you will be destroyed for not obeying*
*the Lord your God."*

Moses knew the importance of remembering the way God
had provided for the nation of Israel's needs, especially
during the 40 years wandering in the wilderness, especially
in the hard times. He understood that human beings
have a tendency to forget the goodness of God and the
ways He blesses our lives. He understood the human
tendency to go from a God-focused nation to a me-focused
individual. And the way to combat it was to be thankful
and to remember. Unfortunately, just a few generations
later Israel forgot the goodness of God and saw only their
momentary success and comfort. They became me-focused
when they should have realized that everything they had
was a gift from God.

Think about your own life for a moment. **What things has
God done in your life in the past year that were "WOW
God" moments?** We all have them, but unless we write
them down, they are easy to forget. This past year has
been a year of WOW God moments for me, and thankfully
I have a lot of them written down in my thankfulness
journal. This year God called me to step out of the full-
time ministry I had been working with for almost six
years to start pursuing my calling and passion. He laid the
foundation for me to write this book. He gave me women

who have already been where I am now to be mentors in my life. He provided financially for me when I quit my income-producing job. He gave me free housing as I travel across the country for three months. And there are so many more HUGE things He has done.

**What about you? What things has God done in your life that were evidence of His love and care for you?** Start writing them down because I can guarantee, down the road when you slip into becoming me-focused, you will need a reminder.

Here are a few tips to help you get started:
1. **Purchase a cute, fun journal that you LOVE to get out and write in.**
2. **Keep it in a place that is visible and easily accessible.**
3. **Write in it often. I would suggest, as you start your thankfulness practice, you write in it every day.**
4. **Start with even the small things or the things you take for granted.**
   - *Thank you God for giving me air to breath.*
   - *Thank you God for a furnace in the winter.*
   - *Thank you God for a body that can walk and move.*
5. **Read through it and remind yourself of the things you are thankful for at least once a week.**

This practice has the ability to transform your day-to-day life. It has the ability to change your attitude in just an instant. You know the saying, "Thankful people are happy people!" It's true. When you are thankful, even on the days that start out badly, you have the ability to see beyond your bad circumstances and feel joy. It's one of the reasons that God's Word talks about thankfulness and gratitude so often.

Our natural state as human beings is to be the opposite of thankful. We look at life's circumstances and see all of the worst things that are happening. We view our lives through the lens of our me-mindedness, and it destroys our joy. When we see these things creeping in and stealing our joy, it's time to refocus. Galatians 5 not only talks about the fruit of the Spirit, but it also talks about our natural state as human beings apart from the Spirit.

> ### Galatians 5:16-25
> "So I say, walk by the Spirit, and you will not gratify the desires of the flesh. 17 For the flesh desires what is contrary to the Spirit, and the Spirit what is contrary to the flesh. They are in conflict with each other, so that you are not to do whatever you want.
> 18 But if you are led by the Spirit, you are not under the law. 19 The acts of the flesh are obvious: sexual immorality, impurity and debauchery;
> 20 idolatry and witchcraft; hatred, discord, jealousy, fits of rage, selfish ambition, dissensions, factions 21 and envy; drunkenness, orgies, and the like. I warn you, as I did before, that those who live like this will not inherit the kingdom of God.
> 22 But the fruit of the Spirit is love, joy, peace, forbearance, kindness, goodness, faithfulness, 23 gentleness and self-control. Against such things there is no law.

*24 Those who belong to Christ Jesus have crucified the flesh with its passions and desires.*
*25 Since we live by the Spirit, let us keep in step with the Spirit."*

Let's look at the contrasting verses in the passage of scripture. While Galatians 5 doesn't focus specifically on gratitude and thankfulness, we can see how the principle is evident throughout. The first thing we notice is the contrast between the Spirit and the flesh. This is what I call God-mindedness and me-mindedness. **The Spirit is the antithesis of our natural desires.** God's Spirit dwelling in us makes us crave and desire what is contrary to our human nature. But unless we are aware of it and are cultivating a renewed mind and walking in the Spirit, our natural tendency is to go toward me-mindedness.

What things does this verse say are the works of the flesh?

| | |
|---|---|
| SEXUAL IMMORALITY | IMPURITY |
| DEBAUCHERY | IDOLATRY |
| WITCHCRAFT | HATRED |
| DISCORD | JEALOUSY |
| FITS OF RAGE | SELFISH AMBITION |
| DISSENSIONS | FACTIONS |
| ENVY | DRUNKENNESS |
| ORGIES | AND THE LIKE... |

I think we all agree that all of those things are bad character traits. And if you are anything like me, you are reading through that list checking off all the things you are NOT. I'm not a sexual deviant...check. Idolatry...I don't have a gold statue in my house that I worship...check.

Debauchery...what is that? Well I guess if I don't know what it is I can't be doing it...check. Witchcraft...does being a part of House Gryffindor count?...maybe check? Hatred...I don't think I hate anyone right now...check. Fits of rage...as long as I don't count that road rage last week... check. We go through the list justifying our guilt, because we know there are things on this list that fit us to a tee.

Then we contrast it with the fruit of the Spirit:

| | |
|---|---|
| LOVE | JOY |
| PEACE | PATIENCE |
| KINDNESS | GOODNESS |
| FAITHFULNESS | GENTLENESS |
| SELF-CONTROL | |

...AGAINST SUCH THERE IS NO LAW.

We don't tend to compare ourselves with this list in the same way as the last one, do we? These are all the things that we have been taught since Sunday school that we should be all the time. All these things are evidence of the indwelling Spirit of God working in our lives. We hope that all of these things are things that define us as believers, but deep down we realize that some of those other things from the first list hold a pretty prominent place in our lives, like jealousy, envy, dissension, idolatry, hatred, factions... things that come up in our lives more often than we would like to admit.

Thankfulness, specifically thankfulness to God, has a way of mitigating those negative things we wish we could avoid. Thankfulness leads us to God and away from our self-focus. It brings us to the feet of Jesus in worship. In general, we aren't thankful for things we have done for ourselves. **Gratitude comes from things outside of ourselves and helps us to remember that it's not all about us.**

There are a few things that are good indicators of our lack of gratitude and thankfulness. They are things that just don't mesh with the Spirit of God in our lives. When we see these things come up, it's usually a pretty good indicator of our focus on self rather than on God and others.

## A CRITICAL SPIRIT

What is a critical spirit? A "critical spirit" is an obsessive attitude of criticism and fault-finding which seeks to tear down others rather than build up. It's something that human beings in general struggle with. Often a critical spirit comes from a place of either insecurity or pride in our identity. We want people to understand our intentions, but when it comes to others, we judge them based solely on their actions. Having a critical spirit is the opposite of meekness, patience, kindness, and gentleness.

> *Romans 14:10-13*
> *"You, then, why do you judge your brother or sister? Or why do you treat them with contempt? For we will all stand before God's judgment seat.*
> *11 It is written:*
> > *"'As surely as I live,' says the Lord,*
> > *'every knee will bow before me;*
> > *every tongue will acknowledge God.'"*

*12 So then, each of us will give an account of ourselves to God. 13 Therefore let us stop passing judgment on one another. Instead, make up your mind not to put any stumbling block or obstacle in the way of a brother or sister."*

## SELF-CENTEREDNESS

Self-centeredness is the pursuit of gratification from vain or egotistical admiration of one's perfect or ideal self-image and attributes. This is a big one that we see everywhere in our world today. It's actually often thought to be self-confidence. But I bet each and every one of us can think of a person that is FAR beyond the realm of confidence. They are about themselves and their own desires all the time. Jesus is the perfect example for us of the opposite of self-centeredness which is love, goodness, gentleness, and meekness.

### Philippians 2:1-8

*"Therefore, if you have any encouragement from being united with Christ, if any comfort from his love, if any common sharing in the Spirit, if any tenderness and compassion, 2 then make my joy complete by being like-minded, having the same love, being one in spirit and of one mind. 3 Do nothing out of selfish ambition or vain conceit. Rather, in humility value others above yourselves, 4 not looking to your own interests but each of you to the interests of the others.*
*5 In your relationships with one another, have the same mindset as Christ Jesus:*
*6 Who, being in very nature God, did not consider equality with God something to be used to his own*

*advantage; 7 rather, he made himself nothing by taking the very nature of a servant, being made in human likeness. 8 And being found in appearance as a man, he humbled himself by becoming obedient to death— even death on a cross!"*

## BITTERNESS

Bitterness affects our soul in a way that nothing else does. Bitterness or resentment have a way of infiltrating every aspect of our lives. Focusing continually on the person or situation we view as negative, a hatred grows and spreads throughout our life. Bitterness is like a slow-working poison that over time has a fatal ending. It's a growing epidemic in our society as our me-mindedness takes over. If we perceive someone is treating us unfairly, they go into the grudge pile. We even have sayings that teach us to hold onto bitterness and resentment. "Fool me once, shame on you; fool me twice, shame on me." Jesus and the Bible teach the exact opposite. The opposite of bitterness is first and foremost forgiveness, but also love, joy, peace, patience, and kindness.

### Matthew 18:21-35
*"Then Peter came to Jesus and asked, "Lord, how many times shall I forgive my brother or sister who sins against me? Up to seven times?"*
*22 Jesus answered, "I tell you, not seven times, but seventy-seven times.*
*23 "Therefore, the kingdom of heaven is like a king who wanted to settle accounts with his servants. 24 As he began the settlement, a man who owed him ten thousand bags of gold was brought to him. 25 Since*

*he was not able to pay, the master ordered that he and his wife and his children and all that he had be sold to repay the debt.*

*26 "At this the servant fell on his knees before him. 'Be patient with me,' he begged, 'and I will pay back everything.' 27 The servant's master took pity on him, canceled the debt and let him go.*

*28 "But when that servant went out, he found one of his fellow servants who owed him a hundred silver coins. He grabbed him and began to choke him. 'Pay back what you owe me!' he demanded. 29 "His fellow servant fell to his knees and begged him, 'Be patient with me, and I will pay it back.' 30 "But he refused. Instead, he went off and had the man thrown into prison until he could pay the debt. 31 When the other servants saw what had happened, they were outraged and went and told their master everything that had happened.*

*32 "Then the master called the servant in. 'You wicked servant,' he said, 'I canceled all that debt of yours because you begged me to. 33 Shouldn't you have had mercy on your fellow servant just as I had on you?' 34 In anger his master handed him over to the jailers to be tortured, until he should pay back all he owed.*

*35 "This is how my heavenly Father will treat each of you unless you forgive your brother or sister from your heart."*

## DISCONTENTMENT

Discontentment is a desire for something one does not have, or being unsatisfied with life because it's not what you hoped or dreamed it would be. Discontentment comes from a lack of gratitude and thankfulness. And discontentment has a tendency to grow far beyond itself and infiltrate all areas of your life. In a society that tells us that we deserve to be treated well and have all the nicest things even when we are not willing to do the work, discontentment runs rampant. Discontentment is the opposite of thankfulness, gratitude, joy, and sometimes self-control.

> **Philippians 4:11-13**
> *"I am not saying this because I am in need, for I have learned to be content whatever the circumstances. 12 I know what it is to be in need, and I know what it is to have plenty. I have learned the secret of being content in any and every situation, whether well fed or hungry, whether living in plenty or in want. 13 I can do all this through him who gives me strength."*

The title of this chapter is "Cultivate Thankfulness", which I thought was fitting because of what the word cultivate means. I got this definition from vocabulary.com and thought it would be the perfect close to this chapter.

To cultivate is to **nurture and help grow.**
Farmers cultivate crops, fundraising
professionals cultivate donors, and
celebrities cultivate their images.
When you cultivate something,
**you work to make it better.** Originally, the word referred only to crops that required tilling, but the meaning has widened. **No matter what is being cultivated, the word implies a level of care that is**

*reminiscent of gardening.* Sometimes friendships come naturally and sometimes you have to cultivate them. To cultivate anything requires *an attention to detail, an understanding of what is being cultivated, and a lot of patience.*

When we take the time and care to cultivate an attitude of thankfulness and gratitude, it changes our perspective. It makes us look outside of ourselves and our circumstances and points us to God. It creates in us a longing for love, joy, peace, patience, kindness, goodness, faithfulness, gentleness, and self-control. **Thankfulness draws us closer to the things of God and allows us to find joy in even the most difficult of circumstances.**

So for today, I will choose to be thankful. How about you?

# CHAPTER FIVE

# RENEW
# YOUR MIND

I am going to start this chapter by giving you a glimpse into the mind of a person who was a slave to an eating disorder, specifically me. I figure, if I lay my soul bare, you may have an easier time exposing yours to the light of day. As you will see, the process of renewing your mind is a brutal one, but SO worth it. It will bring to light things that have been hidden in the dark recesses of your mind for years, and it will also give you hope. It will be painful and sometimes feel awful, but it will bring healing in ways you can't imagine. I am sure throughout this book you have already seen a glimpse of the craziness that was my mind, but believe me when I tell you, we are just getting started.

At the beginning of my journey, I started a freedom journal, writing down my thoughts anytime I felt overcome by emotion or when I wanted to shut down because of the pain. For those that know me, this is not normal for me. I am naturally a level-headed, logical, confident person; but after being beaten down by an eating disorder for so many years, I was barely a shadow of my normal self. This is an entry from the second week of my journey to be free.

> *I feel like I am drowning in my own mind right now.*
> *Through this process of calling out my thoughts, I am*
> *overwhelmed by the emotions and anxiety I feel. I*
> *never knew these thoughts were so engrained in my*
> *head. Plus, I've never cried so much in my entire life.*
> *I am exhausted from battling my thoughts this week;*
> *but even though I am worn down, I see a light growing,*
> *and hope for the first time in a long time. This week*
> *I came to the shocking realization that I am terrified*
> *to find out who I am without my eating disorder. It's*

*crazy that the thing I hate most is the thing I believe is the only thing I am. My eating disorder is my identity, and I HATE that. I know I am so much more than it has made me, but I am terrified to find out who that is. What if I hate the person I am without it?*

*Today I had the thought, "I am not worth loving, I should probably eat. Food makes me feel loved." I can't believe that is even something that I think about myself. How long have I felt I was unworthy of love? How long have I degraded myself because of my lack of control with food? I am noticing a very strong pattern of thought in my life right now and it goes something like this: "I am tired...I should eat." "I feel overwhelmed...I should eat." "I feel anxious...I should eat." "I am bored...I should eat." "I need to diet...I should eat all the things until I start that diet." It seems like every thought I have is turned back into a way to use food as a crutch instead of dealing with the real problem.*

*Then there are the darker thoughts that creep into my mind that I never even knew existed: "Food is my comfort, I run to it when I need to feel loved." "I can protect myself from ever being hurt again by eating a lot of food." Eventually my thoughts reveal that food has very little to do with the insecurity I feel about myself. "You are disgusting, how could anyone ever love you?" "You are a disappointment to God and people around you." "Life is easier when you don't put yourself out there." "As long as you hide you will be safe."*

*Today I am speaking truth over my life, even if I don't believe it right now...NONE OF THOSE THINGS ARE TRUE. I am created by a God that doesn't make mistakes. I am worthy of love and AM LOVED. I desire to be known and loved fully, and that cannot happen if I hide. God is my comfort in times of trouble, not food.*

I hope sharing this with you will help you see my heart in writing this book. Looking back at this, I am reminded of the desperation I felt. I was not alone, but I felt like I was. For you, it may not be food that you use as a crutch in your life to feel loved and accepted. For another woman I know, the need to do good things and gain the approval of others was a big struggle. She wrongly believed that if she could just do enough good things that her life would be worth something. I have met many women who are desperate to feel something other than what they feel right now. They keep running to the same destructive things over and over again, just like I did with food. And until we realize that the only place worth running is straight to God and His promises and love, we will continue feeling this way.

This chapter is the MEAT of this book. It is the answer to what you have been searching for. It will help take you from floundering and desperate to confident and called. My promise to you is, if you put these principles into practice, you will see change take place. You will begin to overcome the lies in your head and will finally be ready to step into your God-calling with purpose and passion. I believe that wholeheartedly because that is exactly what it did in my life.

In chapter 2, we talked about the foundation from God's Word for renewing our mind and meditating. Every concept in this chapter is found in God's Word and is worth embracing wholeheartedly. There will be people who read this book whose lives remain exactly the same; but the only way that can happen is if they don't follow through. This book and the process of renewing your mind does no good if you do it for a week and then stop. It is a continual practice that has the ability to transform your mind. It is hope for those who feel hopeless. It is new life for those who feel desperate.

These are God's principles, found and taught throughout God's Word. **His Word is the place where our minds will truly be transformed and healed.** I went to a conference recently that focused on the names and promises of God as found in the Bible. It was like breathing life into my bones as I realized that God's Word is my truth when I am battling the storms of life. The answers and truth can't come from my own greatness; they need to come from something outside of myself. My truth (from within) has a tendency to waiver when it's not built on the foundation of the Bible.

As we jump into the main material of this chapter, I want to remind you of something we talked about earlier. These principles have the ability to change your outlook on life and thereby change your life. Our brains are masters at changing naturally on their own; but when we tell our brains to change, there is naturally going to be kick back. You will feel uncomfortable...often. You will doubt whether it's actually going to work. You will probably feel fear throughout this process. You will probably even wonder at times if it's worth it. I have seen that scenario play out over and over again in the lives of women. They believe these principles can change their life, BUT they are afraid what change would look like. So they play it safe. They follow the steps, but they don't commit to them. They follow through with their actions (for a while), but they don't do it wholeheartedly. Don't be that person. Commit to being an all-in person. You would not be reading this book if you didn't want to change and grow and be free, right?

## RENEW YOUR MIND

### THE FOUR STEPS ARE SIMPLE.
1. SEE YOUR THOUGHTS.
2. SAY YOUR THOUGHTS.
3. SPEAK TRUTH.
4. SET YOUR MIND.

If you follow me on Instagram or Facebook, you have probably noticed my fascination with old buildings and, more specifically, doors. I like to think of life like a house. Imagine with me for a moment a beautiful cottage created by the Master Crafter for you to live in. When it was new, it was by far the most unique and individual piece of art he had ever created because he built it with you in mind. He put thought into each and every aspect of this house. The windows were leaded glass and encased in intricate, beautiful redwood. The floors were hand-planed to show the dedication and skill of the Master. The inside doors were each hand carved, and they opened and closed with precision to beautiful rooms that were an extension of the builder's craftsmanship.

At the heart of the home is a glorious fireplace, designed
to radiate warmth to every corner of the home, and again
the Master placed His hand-carved artwork on it. Every
part of the home was to His exact specifications, and each
aspect was thought out with love and care. The most
masterful creation and the thing that took the most time was
the creation of the front door. He spent countless hours
putting His special touch into the front door. He created a
door that people loved to look at and couldn't wait to open
to discover what lay beyond the threshold. It was truly the
thing that defined and proclaimed the beauty of the home
that was within.

When he is finished with it, he hands you the keys with
pride and tells you that he cannot wait for you to enjoy
it. But as the years pass, you start taking for granted the
unique touches placed in that home. At some point the
floor boards get water damage, and the fireplace gets
covered in soot. The doors creak loudly as they open,
and the paint begins to peel off the walls. The windows,
although cared for when new, become cloudy from years
of misuse. The front door, which once proclaimed the
beauty and skill of the Master, has become rarely used and
neglected. It no longer welcomes people into the home,
because the home has fallen into disrepair. It no longer
reflects the purpose of the Master, because it has not been
maintained to do so.

The Psalmist said in Psalm 139 that you were knit together
in your mother's womb and that God fearfully and
wonderfully made you. We were created for purpose; and
just like that house, God (the Master Builder) perfectly
crafted you to reflect His skill and glory. Nobody in their

right mind would look at that house and tell you what an amazing master crafter YOU are, would they? No, they would want to know who your builder was, and you would happily and boldly declare His name.

**When God created you, He made you to reflect and pursue your purpose. You were exactly the way you were meant to be. Your unique character and personality was handcrafted by God. He knew exactly what He was doing when He knit you together.**

The problem comes when you begin to care for and maintain the life you have been given. Instead of going back to the Master Crafter when something breaks or is in need of repair, you either ignore it or try to fix it yourself. Your life falls into disrepair. Instead of allowing God to fix it in you, you close the front door and don't let Him in. You believe you can fix it on your own, yet your fix to a problem is like placing duct tape on a leaky pipe.

If you feel like that house, in disrepair and in need of the Master Crafter to come in and restore what is broken, then you are not alone. Over the past two years I have come into contact with hundreds of women who feel that way. They have no idea where they went off track. They feel broken and in need of repair. Most have no idea for what purpose they were created. They are desperate for a glimpse of hope and have a desire to find their purpose and calling so that they can affect change in this world. The four steps I'm about to show you are the first step toward that reality, when your life can be restored to its original purpose. It is time to let the Master Crafter back in to repair the broken and worn down edges of your life.

## SEE YOUR THOUGHTS

The first and most obvious step to renewing your mind is to
see your thoughts.  It is trickier than it sounds, but it helps
your mind move the destructive thoughts in your head to
the forefront of your mind.  Remember when we talked
about the conscious and subconscious thoughts?  This
practice of searching for and seeing your thoughts is one
that will allow the subconscious thoughts to become seen
and known.

When you start practicing this first step, you will notice
things that you may not have noticed for years.  This
practice activates the reticular activating system.  When
you begin searching your mind for deeply engrained
thought patterns, you will start seeing more beliefs and
insecurities than you ever imagined could be there.

As I started this practice in my own life, it happened
slowly...very slowly.  In fact, I wouldn't say that I began
seeing the REAL destructive thought patterns until my
second week.  It started out as superficial thoughts like,
"You should go look in the fridge for food."  Okay...that's
not super destructive, although not helpful.  That thought
quickly became, "You are bored, so you should go look in
the fridge."  Within two weeks it grew to expose a much
deeper thought I was having, "I'm feeling insecure about
the way I look, and I feel a little bored.  I should go look in
the fridge for something to comfort myself."

Do you see the thought progression there?  Fully seeing
your thoughts is digging through your mind. It is searching

for things you have not seen before, and it takes practice. This leads to the next step.

## SAY YOUR THOUGHTS (OUT LOUD)

This step is crucial to seeing your thoughts rightly. When we talked about the amygdala in the chapter on the brain, we learned that it likes to convince our pre-frontal cortex to make emotional rather than logical decisions. As long as our thoughts stay trapped inside the recesses of our mind and not spoken out loud, we will be unable to view them through the lens of our logical brain.

The main reason we must *SAY OUR THOUGHTS OUT LOUD* is because of the way our brains naturally function. Since the pre-frontal cortex is the part of our brains that controls speech, saying our thoughts out loud will actually jump-start the logical brain. The practice of saying what you are thinking out loud will also allow you to dig deeper into the "seeing your thoughts" step as well. If you have no idea how to do this, and feel like a huge goofball, you are not alone. I actually had an extremely hard time with this. Just know that as long as you allow your thoughts to keep rolling around your head, without saying them out loud, they will continue to have power over you. And that is the problem we are trying to cure, right?

To get you started in saying your thoughts out loud, here is a simple exercise. Start by asking this simple question:

*What things am I thinking right now?*

Then start saying everything that pops into your head.

- *The weather is so nice and fallish! I can't wait to wear my beanie.*
- *What things are on my to-do list today?*
- *I feel insecure right now.*
- *I should eat healthy today.*
- *I feel like I am running on empty today.*
- *This day is off to a difficult start.*

Anytime you start seeing thoughts that say things like **I FEEL** or **I SHOULD** that's a good indication that it's a thought worth digging into. Our brains have a tendency to make us do things that we believe or feel. As you begin to notice those buzzwords, you will begin to dig deeper into your thought patterns.

Once you have your list of thoughts, pick out the ones that seem to have an underlying theme and ask yourself: **Why do I FEEL that way?** Or **Why SHOULD I do that?**

The practice of saying your thoughts out loud is an uncovering practice. I like to think of it as layers of the bed. First you have a throw pillow. It is superficial, not really that useful, and it's just for looks. You have a few of those throw pillows (or throw away thoughts). Next you get to the top layer of blankets. First comes the duvet; it's is more substantial than the throw pillows, and is definitely there to cover up what's underneath (second layer of thoughts). Next comes the comforter, there for our comfort and warmth (think big thoughts or beliefs that we run to often or hold about ourselves or our lives). Underneath the comforter is a smaller blanket for warmth, but it is really the barrier between the comforter and sheet layer (the protective layer). Finally, we get down to the flat sheet layer, (getting closer to the REAL issue) which is thinly veiled to cover the fitted sheet, the thing that covers our entire mattress. (Removing this final layer will unveil the real problem.) I view the mattress as the substantial thought or belief we hold about ourselves (our identity). Every other layer of the bed is meant to make us more comfortable and cover up the mattress. That seems like a silly example; but if you think about it as you say your thoughts out loud, you will find it's a great metaphor to dig deeper into your thought life until it finally comes out at the identity piece (the mattress).

## SPEAK TRUTH

Once you start finding those deeper, more substantial thoughts or beliefs, it is time to either substantiate or replace them. The destructive thought patterns that come up over and over again (insecurity, fear, doubt, identity issues) will either be validated incorrectly in our own minds over and over again or destroyed by truth. **As a believer in Jesus, my source of truth comes from who I am in Christ.** Remember that beautiful cottage the Master Builder made that is your life? That is truth.

The focus on truth is of the utmost importance in the process of renewing your mind. Unless your mind finds evidence to the contrary, it will continue to cling to your already foundational beliefs about yourself and this world. Throughout scripture we are called to be people who search for truth. This morning in my study, I read Psalm 1, which illustrates this concept perfectly.

*Psalm 1:1-3*
*"Blessed is the one*
*who does not **walk in step with the wicked***
*or **stand in the way that sinners** take*
*or **sit in the company of mockers**,*
*2 but whose delight is in the law of the Lord,*
*and who meditates on his law day and night.*
*3 That person is like a tree planted by streams of water,*
*which yields its fruit in season*
*and whose leaf does not wither—*
*whatever they do prospers."*

Did you notice the natural progression of the person we
are called **NOT** to be in Psalm 1:1? I bolded it so you can
see it. First it begins by him WALKING in step with the
wicked. Next, as he becomes more comfortable, we see
him STANDING in the way of sinners. And lastly, we
see him SITTING in the company of mockers. He has
stopped on his forward progression and has made himself
comfortable in the place that is the worst for him.

The second verse in this chapter describes the BLESSED
man we see in verse one. He is someone who delights in
the law of the Lord and meditates on His Word throughout
the day. The blessed man is continually being fed truth,
and just like a tree that is planted by a river, he is in a state
of constant growth. He is one whose foundation is firm;
and because of it, he produces the fruit that God desires of
him. And the last thing we see of him is that WHATEVER
he does prospers. However, without the truth of God's
Word, he is likely to fall into the trap of the first man in
verse one who makes his dwelling place surrounded by
enemies.

We already looked at the foundations for renewing our minds in chapter 2, but the unwavering commitment to believing truth in our lives is the key to changing our limiting and destructive belief patterns.

Let's put this into an easy plan to follow. Once you have found the thoughts that are most destructive in your life and that are holding you back and beating you down, and you have said them out loud for your logical brain to hear, it is time to seek truth. Search for the promises of God that are in direct conflict to the thought you have in your head. Search for evidence in your life that is contrary to your pattern of belief. Once you find the truth you are searching for, WRITE IT DOWN and repeat it to yourself often. Our brains have a tendency to forget and fall back on the patterns we have firmly established in our minds. This step of speaking truth needs to be put into our heads over and over again. The point of this exercise is to replace what is not serving us with new, true thought patterns that will build up and restore us.

## SET YOUR MIND.

Whether or not you believe the truth right now at this very moment, the last step in this process is to set your mind. Setting your mind is the act of deciding to believe God rather than yourself. As we have seen throughout this process, your mind lies to you regularly. Your mind has been trained by your insecurities and past hurts and by things other people may have said about you in the past. The good news is that **what God says about you is the thing you are meant to believe and should be believing.**

Renewing your mind is a process that will become more natural as you walk through these steps over and over again in your life. It will be the thing that will free you up to finally step into the freedom God promises in His Word. It is the thing that will allow you to finally live that "abundant life" God wants for you but you never see in your life personally. The act of setting your mind on truth is an intentional act of submission. It is believing that who you are according to God far outweighs who you view yourself to be.

I was amazed by this practice when I first started renewing my mind. At first it felt superficial and fake. Honestly, it felt like I was lying to myself every day. I remember very clearly the day that I finally believed the truths I was setting my mind on. I was sitting in my living room getting ready to teach a women's retreat. It was the first one I had ever done on my own, and I was terrified that I would fail. I was sure that my confidence in my message was ill founded. So I gave myself a pep talk. It went something like this.

> ***Britney Renae Thompson*** *(Yes, I use my full name when I speak to myself)****, you have been called by God to preach truth to the broken-hearted. You have been equipped as a workmanship of God to do good works which God established for you to do before the foundation of the earth. You are fearfully and wonderfully made. You are a woman who longs to bring to light the heart of God to a hurting and perverse generation. You are called, gifted, and crafted by the Master Potter to be a vessel of honor and glory for His good pleasure. You are not alone.***

*God is with you, whatever you do or wherever you go.
You are dearly loved and confidently called to glorify
the name of Jesus to these women. Now go do it!*

From that point on I believed those things about myself
100%. The coolest part about that pep talk was that almost
every single one of those truths are truths found in God's
Word. The pep talk was not in my own ability or greatness;
it wasn't built upon a sandy foundation. It was built upon
the foundation of God's Word, a solid foundation of truth.
That day I set my mind to go after my God-calling even
when I was scared or feeling insecure.

Setting your mind is something that must be done often and
regularly. I know I keep saying this but it is because I want
you to grasp its importance. Just like seeing your thoughts,
saying your thoughts, and speaking truth are intentional
actions that are meant to renew your mind and reset your
brain, so is setting your mind. Unless you commit to
setting your mind on truth and never wavering, you will be
like the person described in Ephesians 4 who doesn't know
their calling and is immature in their faith.

### Ephesians 4:11-16

*11 "And it was He who gave some to be apostles, some
to be prophets, some to be evangelists, and some to be
pastors and teachers, 12 to equip the saints for works
of ministry, to build up the body of Christ, 13 until we
all reach unity in the faith and in the knowledge of the
Son of God, as we mature to the full measure of the
stature of Christ.
14 Then we will no longer be infants, tossed about
by the waves and carried around by every wind of*

*teaching and by the clever cunning of men in their deceitful scheming. 15 Instead, speaking the truth in love, we will in all things grow up into Christ Himself, who is the head. 16 From Him the whole body, fitted and held together by every supporting ligament, grows and builds itself up in love through the work of each individual part."*

God gave each one of us a unique gifting and calling and calls us to mature in our faith. As long as we continue setting our minds on the things of God, we will not be like infants who are tossed about by the ways of this world, or more importantly, the waves of our mind. We are meant to live a life of purpose that comes from understanding who we were uniquely created to be.

I want to finish this chapter by speaking truth into your mind and life. When you are feeling beat up and beat down by your thoughts or are wondering if it will ever get better, you can use these promises of God to speak truth to yourself. When you are in Christ, you don't have to wonder if God's desire is for you to be healed and free. **It most certainly is!**

As you read through these verses, take some time to write out your declaration of truth like I did above. I included some lines at the end of this chapter for you to speak truth to yourself. I don't know the things you struggle with personally, but God does. Speak truth over your life in the lines below by filling them up with promises of who God says who you are, what He created you for, and the ways He desires to use and bless you. Then post these promises in a place where you will see them often. Remember, it is not about who YOU ARE but about who God IS and has called you to be. A great promise to start with is this: "I am a unique and deeply loved creation of the Almighty God." I got you started; now you get to decide for yourself the truth you need to set your mind on today.

## WHEN YOU FEEL ALONE:

### Deuteronomy 31:6
*"Be strong and courageous. Do not be afraid or terrified because of them, for the Lord your God goes with you; he will never leave you nor forsake you."*

### John 14:16
*"And I will ask the Father, and he will give you another advocate to help you and be with you forever."*

## WHEN YOU FEEL BEATEN DOWN:

### Exodus 14:14
*"The LORD will fight for you; you need only to be still."*

### Psalm 46:1b
*"God is our refuge and strength, an ever-present help in trouble."*

### Isaiah 40:28-31
*"Do you not know?*
*Have you not heard?*
*The Lord is the everlasting God,*
*the Creator of the ends of the earth.*
*He will not grow tired or weary,*

*and his understanding no one can fathom.*
*29 He gives strength to the weary*
*and increases the power of the weak.*
*30 Even youths grow tired and weary,*
*and young men stumble and fall;*
*31 but those who hope in the Lord*
*will renew their strength.*
*They will soar on wings like eagles;*
*they will run and not grow weary,*
*they will walk and not be faint."*

## WHEN YOU ARE AFRAID:

**Isaiah 43:1b**
*"Do not fear, for I have redeemed you;*
*I have summoned you by name; you are mine."*

**1 John 4:16-18**
*"And so we know and rely on the love God has*
*for us. God is love. Whoever lives in love lives in*
*God, and God in them. 17 This is how love is made*
*complete among us so that we will have confidence on*
*the day of judgment: In this world we are like Jesus.*
*18 There is no fear in love. But perfect love drives out*
*fear, because fear has to do with punishment. The one*
*who fears is not made perfect in love."*

**Joshua 1:9**
*"Have I not commanded you? Be strong and*
*courageous. Do not be afraid; do not be discouraged,*
*for the Lord your God will be with you wherever*
*you go."*

# WHEN YOU FEEL INSECURE:

### Psalm 139:13,14
"For You formed my inward parts;
You wove me in my mother's womb.
14 I will give thanks to You, for I am fearfully
and wonderfully made;
Wonderful are Your works,
And my soul knows it very well."

### Philippians 1:6
"...being confident of this, that he who began a good
work in you will carry it on to completion until the day
of Christ Jesus."

# DECLARATION OF TRUTH

Barbara Johnson

*You are a unique and deeply loved creation
of the almighty God.*

I am Fearfully and wonderfully made I was knitted in my mothers womb. Your works are wonderful. I have been chosen and he works out everything with his purpose. He has marked me with a seal I am the daughter of the king I am Confident he began a good work in me and will see it to completion

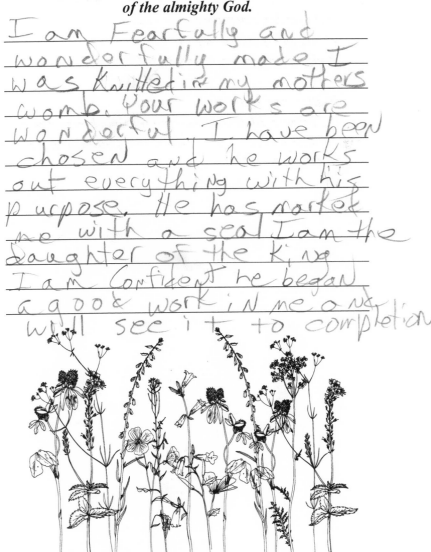

# CHAPTER SIX

# EMOTIONAL FALL-OUT

I purposefully waited to write this chapter until after all the other chapters were written (including the two chapters that follow). I thought I had left it until the end because it would be one of the easiest chapters to finish. The material I prepared to put into this chapter was straight forward, easy to follow, and was the logical next step to follow the chapter you just finished reading. Little did I know that God had a plan and purpose for this chapter beyond my understanding and planning.

This morning when I woke up, I knew this was the day I had set aside to FINISH the writing of God-Minded. It has been a date on my calendar for awhile now and was always an ever-approaching target. I knew that today would be a day of great change and excitement as I finally finished this huge project. I couldn't wait to move on to the more creative aspects of this project and the other things I was placing on the back burner until after I was finished with God-Minded.

As I have worked through this process of renewing my mind day after day for two years, I am still shocked by the way my brain responds to certain things. Today was one of those days. I woke up FEELING as though I would like to sleep in on this day because it was going to be a big day. I woke up knowing that I SHOULD take some time for myself this morning because, let's be honest, I have worked really hard. I woke up with a sense of foreboding that comes when big change is evident in my life. Did you notice those buzzwords FEELING and SHOULD? As I lay in bed far longer than I needed to, I began saying my thoughts out loud. The conversation went something like this:

*"Britney you have so much to get done today. Why not take some time to just relax?"*

*"If you relax, then you can tackle that chapter when you are good and rested."* (Note: I had just had one of the best night's sleep of my life.)

*"I feel like I don't really want to write today. Maybe I should work on a different project."*

*"Yeah, that's a good idea. What if I put off the writing until tomorrow when I feel more up to it?"*

*"No, I really want to meet my deadline. I should get up and write."*

*"But if you write it today then you will be done... what's next?"*

**And the final thought that woke me up to the truth of my reason for procrastination was this one:**

*"If you finish this book today then this ministry is really going to happen. Finishing this book means there is no turning back."*

The crazy thing throughout this interaction with my thoughts this morning is that I was able to overcome a fear that had been lingering in the back of my mind for who knows how long. My neurotic brain was still clinging to the hope that things would eventually "go back to normal." Now I don't know about you, but I have no desire to go back to my brain's version of normal. It was a place where I felt trapped, alone, and unworthy. My normal for most of my adult life was feeling judged and insignificant. Why in the world would I want to go back to that place?

Change is inevitable in life, and it's our responsibility to teach our brains how to react when those big things come

109

up. This process of renewing your mind is one of those big changes that will leave your brain reeling. The natural kickback that will happen is normally bigger than just fear and doubt, but those are the biggest ones you will start to see. **Your brain will do everything in its power to convince you that changing is the worst thing you could possibly do.** It will do its best to show you that renewing your mind is the craziest thing you have ever tried to do in your entire life. It will make you feel at times like you have gone crazy. And that's a good thing…it means that our brains are functioning the way God created them to.

The emotional response that happens in our brains due to change is fascinating. Elizabeth Kugler-Ross wrote a book on dealing with death and dying in 1969. She laid out a module of dealing with big changes or life shattering loss. It is widely accepted as an effective way to work through the grief process in the midst of tragic loss. The five stages are: 1) Denial 2) Anger 3) Bargaining 4) Depression 5) Acceptance. While it was originally written as a way to deal with grief, it has been proven over and over as a method to deal with any big changes we make in life. As you start renewing your mind, keep these stages in mind. You will be amazed how closely your thought process will mimic the same pattern as dealing with grief or great loss. Our brains are wired to respond this way in order to keep a sense of normalcy in life.

The thing we need to remember is what "normal" has been for most of our lives. In the midst of the blooming hope of change, it's likely that you feel a growing dread—a growing dread of the unknown. In fact, as you read this chapter and are beginning to put into practice the principles you have learned, you may already be feeling that uneasiness in your spirit. Have you noticed it yet? Our brains are masters of creating normalcy and helping us walk through the process of natural change. It is what our brains were created to do. God created our brains to walk us through infancy, through the teenage years, college years, middle age, and even prepare us and our bodies for old age and finally death. Our brains do all of those things so well; and yet when huge changes arise, for lack of a better term, they "freak out." Anything outside of the planned schedule of events throws the entire system out of whack.

For a person who has struggled with insecurity and identity from childhood, the idea of having a purpose and identity that is secure upsets the natural process. The thing I want you to realize more than anything else is that renewing our minds changes our identity. Now it actually doesn't change our identity as God created us to be. It changes our perceived identity, the one our brain has fostered and cared for all our lives.

## OVERCOMING FEAR AND DOUBT

Two of the most common emotional responses to change are fear and doubt. You will begin to feel these almost instantaneously as you begin renewing your mind. You will also begin to feel things like hope, happiness, and purpose. Don't discount those emotions you feel as fear and doubt arise. Fear has a way of feeling bigger than all of the other emotions. It is our brain's way to protect us when it senses we may be in trouble. The best way to combat fear and doubt is by using the third step of renewing your mind: **Speak truth.**

Do you remember the absolute terror and fear as a child when you woke up from a bad dream? Or when you would convince yourself that there was a monster in the closet? As a child, because the logical center of our brain isn't formed yet, we automatically gave in to the fear response created in our amygdala. There is no other response to fear, so we cowered in it. We had no ability to talk ourselves logically through the impossibility of a big green hairy monster hiding in our closet that wanted to eat us, or the craziness of suffocating in a cave that was slowly filling up with popcorn. (A recurring nightmare I had) In fact, we were so convinced of the reliability of our terror that nothing short of our parents' comfort and perceived safety could calm us down. It took something outside of ourselves to calm the fear growing in us. We needed to feel safe, even though we weren't in danger in the first place. Our brains still respond in exactly the same way to those types of overwhelming and terrifying thoughts:

*"You won't be yourself anymore if you get rid of your eating disorder."*

*"The man that is abusing you is the only man who will love you. You cannot live without him. Maybe he will change."*

*"Quitting your job and moving across the country will leave you homeless and with no friends. You should stay in your hometown until you die."*

*"Until you are married, you will always be lacking something. You need a man to make your life complete."*

*"Without my children I am nobody. I had better hold on to them tighter and make them more dependent on me so they will never leave me."*

Do you notice the fear tactic in each one of those thoughts? Do you see the illogical thought that follows? The pattern isn't hard to recognize when you see it written down here. But how much more difficult is it to see when those thoughts are swirling around in your own mind? Fear and doubt will always tout themselves as "logical thought" and will do their best to convince you that what is best for you is to stay exactly the same as you are right now. The problem with that is that change is inevitable. Change will happen for the better or the worse. You get to decide which one it is.

## PRACTICE MAKES PERMANENT

We are told from the time we are young that practice makes perfect. Band teachers recite that as we pick up our first instruments and begin playing. We are told that by coaches as we start a new sport. We are told that by teachers as we hone our math or writing skills. But the truth of the matter is that "perfection" is an unachievable goal. No matter how much we practice our instruments, we will always make mistakes. No matter how good we are at math, there will always be another unsolvable equation. No matter how good we are at basketball, we will still miss shots. The idea of perfection is so attractive. What would it be like to finally get to the place where we no longer make mistakes, when we can finally be free of failure? It's enticing.

I want you to get this...so please listen.

**Perfection is a lie Satan loves to trap you in.** It will keep you stuck and make you feel insecure. It will make you feel like a failure, and you will live a disappointed life. If you step into this process with the mindset that you are going to do it perfectly and never fall back into your old patterns, you will fail miserably and feel defeated in the process. The process of renewing your mind is a messy and sanctifying process. While you tear down the strongholds your mind has created in your life, you also need to build up truth strongholds. **Renewing your mind is meant to be messy; it's meant to teach you how to rise from the ashes of a burned down life with the prospect of the life God created you to live.** The goal in renewing your mind is to make it so normal that it becomes a permanent stronghold. So what if you changed the quote from "practice makes perfect" to a more realistic and hope filled "PRACTICE MAKES PERMANENT?"

Having something that is permanent in life gives a sense of normalcy and hope. It gives the ability to have something to lean back on when feeling lost and alone. Thankfully for those of us who are believers, we have someone that is both permanent and PERFECT in our lives. He can be our place to run to when we are feeling on shaky ground. In the midst of fear and doubt, He becomes our safety and our place of comfort. We were never meant to do this life alone. Thankfully, when we are in Christ, we are given the gift of the Holy Spirit who is our comforter and our hope. There is no question that God wants the best for our lives. There is no fear that we will wake up one day to discover that God does not love us anymore. When doubts arise over our insecurities, the place we need to run is to God and His promises. When we feel lost and alone, we need to be reminded that we are never alone because the Lord our God is with us wherever we go.

Speaking truth in the midst of crushing fear and doubt removes the pressure from our own perfectionist mindset. We have the ability to renew our minds because of the shed blood of Jesus on the cross for our sins and the reconciliation we now have. When I forget my place and feel lost and hurt and floundering, these are verses that I read OUT LOUD to speak truth into my life.

> ### Romans 5:1-11
> "Therefore, since **we have been justified through faith, we have peace with God** through our Lord Jesus Christ, 2 through whom we have **gained access by faith into this grace in which we now stand.** And we boast in the hope of the glory of God. 3 Not only so, but we also glory in our sufferings, because we know that suffering produces perseverance; 4 perseverance, character; and character, hope. 5 And hope does not put us to shame, because **God's love has been poured out into our hearts through the Holy Spirit, who has been given to us.** 6 You see, at just the right time, **when we were still powerless, Christ died for the unGodly.** 7 Very rarely will anyone die for a righteous person, though for a good person someone might possibly dare to die. 8 **But God demonstrates his own love for us in this: While we were still sinners, Christ died for us.**
> 9 Since we have now been justified by his blood, how much more shall we be saved from God's wrath through him! 10 For if, **while we were God's enemies, we were reconciled to him through the death of his Son, how much more, having been reconciled, shall we be saved**

*through his life! 11 Not only is this so, but we also boast in God through our Lord Jesus Christ, through whom **we have now received reconciliation.**"*

This, ladies, is truth spoken at its finest. Look at the truth of our identity when contrasted with the character of God. It is so powerful to see that God loves us in spite of ourselves. Notice something as we walk through this passage of scripture written by the Apostle Paul who, by the way, murdered Christians. Notice that every single one of these things we already HAVE in Christ Jesus. This entire passage is written in the past present tense. (It's something that was purchased in the past that we also currently possess.) That means that it is not something we are looking to possess or earn at some point in the future. It's something we CURRENTLY possess. In other words, signed, sealed, and delivered, it's yours.

Here's a quick definition of a few of the words used in this passage.

**JUSTIFIED**: declared or made righteous in the sight of God. One way I like to remember it is this way: **Just as if I had never sinned**.

**RIGHTEOUS**: morally right or justifiable; virtuous. Or I have heard it said this way: Right in God's sight.

**RECONCILED**: The act of restoring us to right relationship with God.

Understand your identity as viewed through the eyes of God. When we walk through the process of renewing our minds, our brains will try to remind us of who WE THINK we are. It will remind us of the person it believes us to be. This identity God gives us as found in Romans 5 is worth more weight than who we believe ourselves to be in our short-sighted beliefs. It's our TRUE identity as someone who believes in Jesus for salvation. It will help us put in alignment our skewed version of ourselves. And through this process of defining our true identity, we will become the person God desires for us to be and has prepared for us to become.

Notice our identity as written in the words of Paul in Romans 5:

1. **We are justified through faith.**
2. **We are at peace with God.**
3. **We have access to God and can now stand.**
4. **We boast in the hope found in God.**
5. **We glory in our suffering, because through it we build perseverance, character and hope.**
6. **We are loved by God, as shown by the gift of the Holy Spirit.**
7. **God knows our sin, and loved us enough to die for us.**
8. **We are justified through Jesus' blood.**
9. **We are saved from God's wrath.**
10. **We WERE (formerly) enemies of God but are now reconciled to God through Jesus.**

If you'll notice, each of these things has very little to do with us. Rather our identity becomes wrapped up in the things God has done for us. He becomes our true identity. He becomes the reason we have hope. He becomes our help in time of need. He is the reason we can overcome fear and doubt. These verses leave NOTHING outside of God's perfect hand on our lives. He is our hope and the firm foundation that we cling to when we are feeling uneasy, lost, and afraid.

We learned in the last chapter the importance of seeing our thoughts, saying them out loud, speaking truth, and setting our minds. **But what happens when our brains tell us that it is not working, that we are wasting our time?** What if we are afraid of the person we will become? As we have established, our brains are masters at convincing us to stay the same. So how do we overcome those crippling fears? Below are a few things you can remind yourself of when self-doubt creeps in. They have become my fallback when I notice my brain making a stink about change.

## 1. GO TO GOD'S WORD.

As you have seen throughout this book, God's Word is FULL of truth. The Bible is God's love story to us. It is His heart, speaks of His identity, and shows us His love for us. From the first couple of chapters in the Bible and on, we see God's desire for relationship with us. We see our need for control ruining that relationship and everything else leading up to the point where that relationship to God would be restored. Through the birth of Jesus, His life on this earth and His death on the cross, we see the full love of God on display: His love for you, His desire for relationship, and His desire for worship.

The Bible should be your go-to tool for renewing your mind and finding your identity and calling. It is trustworthy, and no matter what the world tells you, is historically accurate and worth trusting. God's Word is your main source of information about who your God is and His desire for your life. It is the place you should run to when life doesn't make sense. It is your confidence that, even when life feels like it's falling apart, God is still in control. Remind yourself often to go to God's Word. Don't make it a chore, make it a priority in your life. It is not one more thing to be checked off your list in order to live a righteous life. It's the thing that enables you to live a life worthy of the calling God has given you.

### Hebrews 4:12
*"For the word of God is alive and active. Sharper than any double-edged sword, it penetrates even to dividing soul and spirit, joints and marrow; it judges the thoughts and attitudes of the heart."*

### 2 Timothy 3:16,17
*"All Scripture is God-breathed and is useful for teaching, rebuking, correcting and training in righteousness, so that the servant of God may be thoroughly equipped for every good work."*

### Psalm 119:105
*"Your word is a lamp for my feet, a light on my path."*

### Matthew 7:24
*"Therefore everyone who hears these words of mine and puts them into practice is like a wise man who built his house on the rock."*

### John 8:31, 32
*"To the Jews who had believed him, Jesus said, "If you*

*hold to my teaching, you are really my disciples. Then you will know the truth, and the truth will set you free." "*

## 2. FIND MOTIVATIONAL QUOTES THAT SPEAK TRUTH.

Here are a few of my favorite quotes to remind myself of who I am and who I desire to be. When I feel weak or in need of encouragement, I remind myself of who God says I am. Quotes are an easy way to memorize truths that are important to us.

*"Our God is not fickle, forgetful or fragile in any way. And He does not make mistakes."*
*-Lysa Terkeurst*

*"If our identity is in our work, rather than Christ, success will go to our heads, and failure will go to our hearts."*
*-Timothy Keller*

*"If your identity is found in Christ, then it matters less and less what people think of you."*
*-Leonard I. Sweet*

*"Give God your problems, your fears and your worries. He will guide you and bring you through them for He is good all the time."*
*- Pat Francis*

*"Be Yourself. Everyone else is already taken."*
*-Gilbert Perreira*

## 3. REMIND YOURSELF OF YOUR IDENTITY IN CHRIST.

*I am loved exactly as I am.*
(John 3:1-2, John 3:16, Romans 5:8)
*I am God's child.*
(John 1:12, 1 John 3:1)
*God desires my good.*
(Romans 8:28)
*I am free from shame, fear and guilt.*
(Romans 8:1, Ephesians 1:7, John 8:36)
*I am whole and complete.*
(Colossians 2:10, 1 Peter 2:24, 2 Corinthians 5:21)
*I am called for a purpose.*
(John 15:16, Romans 8:28)
*I am not condemned.*
(Romans 8:1)
*I am no longer a slave to my sin.*
(Romans 6:6)
*I am a conqueror.*
(Romans 8:31-39)
*I am filled with the Holy Spirit.*
(Ephesians 1:13-14, John 14:15-18, I Corinthians 6:19)
*I am His, and I hear His voice.*
(John 10:27-28)
*I am created in His image.*
(Genesis 1:27)
*I am Jesus' friend.*
(John 15:15)

# 4. PRAY

One of the biggest tools we have to fight fear, doubt, and insecurity is prayer. Prayer takes us outside of our circumstances and into the throne room of God. It allows us to empty our heart of fear and doubt and fill it up with the belief that God hears our prayers and will answer. It removes the weight off of our shoulders and places it in the capable hands of God. Prayer is something that we are commanded to do. It is not something that needs to be added to a checklist of daily activities to make us feel more righteous. Praying doesn't make you look any better or more worthy in the eyes of God. It has the ability to calm our minds by reminding us that God is in control.

I have a problem with control, and I think most of us would admit that we struggle with control issues. We like to feel as though we are the masters of our own destiny. We enjoy the feeling of knowing that something is getting done because of our efforts. The problem with control is that when things get out of control, we feel like failures. Control is the opposite of trust.

A great example of this is riding in a car. For me, the experience of sitting in the passenger seat of the car is unsettling. Since I am a single woman in my mid-thirties, I have spent most of the time in the driver's seat of a car. It's very rare that I am not driving. Last week was one of those rare situations, and it became quite evident that my need for control was rearing its ugly head again. As my mom and I made our way through the busy traffic of the city, I kept stomping my foot on the floor of the passenger side of the car and giving unneeded advice until my mom finally said, "Do you just want to drive?" I replied, "No, I'm okay with you driving." Her response was, "Are you sure?" It was a perfect reminder of my control freak mind. In that moment I wanted to say, "Okay I'll drive," but I stopped myself because I realized the ridiculousness of it all. My mother has been driving for many more years than I and has only had one accident that I am aware of (and it wasn't her fault). She is completely capable of handling a car, and yet I was questioning her driving skills at every turn.

How often do we do that with God? We question God's leading in our lives at every turn. We think, in some way, we are the ones who will control the outcome of our lives. We try and try and try to take control that doesn't belong to us. God has promised us in His Word, "His ways are better than ours." (Jeremiah 29:11) And if we "trust in Him, He will make our path straight." (Proverbs 3:5,6) God even promised us, "He will work everything out for our good." (Romans 8:28) Yet even though we know those promises, we still grapple for control of our lives. I like to imagine it is like getting into a car with a blind person who wants to drive. Even though they can't see, they still think they are prepared to get the car to its destination. As they drive down the road, cars are swerving out of the way, and they eventually hit a telephone pole. Instead of taking responsibility for their stupidity, they turn to the passenger and yell, "Why didn't you tell me that was there!?!" That's what it is like when we blame God for the outcome of our actions in our lives.

Prayer is an act of humility and submission to the One who has the ability to control every situation rightly. It's removing our control freak tendency from the equation and laying it at the feet of Jesus. Prayer changes things, not because of anything we have done, but because God is the perfect solution to our weakness. When your mind is going all over the place trying to find a solution to a problem in your life, your natural tendency is to get in the driver's seat blindfolded and make the situation right again. Going to God in prayer is an act of renewing your mind to realize that being in "control" is an illusion. God has the foresight to see the outcome when you are blinded by your circumstances. So take it to God. And when you don't know what to say, allow the Holy Spirit to speak on your behalf. He is your advocate and help when there are no words.

*Romans 8:26-27*
*"In the same way, the Spirit helps us in our weakness. We do not know what we ought to pray for, but the Spirit himself intercedes for us through wordless groans. 27 And he who searches our hearts knows the mind of the Spirit, because the Spirit intercedes for God's people in accordance with the will of God."*

*1 John 5:14, 15*
*"This is the confidence we have in approaching God: that if we ask anything according to his will, he hears us. And if we know that he hears us—whatever we ask—we know that we have what we asked of him."*

*Matthew 26:41*
*"Watch and pray so that you will not fall into temptation. The spirit is willing, but the flesh is weak."*

*Psalm 145:18*
*"The LORD is near to all who call on him, to all who call on him in truth."*

## 5. WORSHIP GOD THROUGH MUSIC

Did you ever get into your car on a really difficult day after work, turn on the radio and a great song comes on that speaks directly to your situation? In the midst of frustration and hard times, music has the ability to lift your soul. For me, it helps when it's a song reminding me of God's goodness. There are a few songs that I have in my arsenal that have become my life anthems. One that spoke to me as I was learning how to renew my mind and overcome fear is by Francesca Battestelli called, "The Break-up Song." It doesn't speak any super deep theological truth, but it is exactly what my soul needs to be reminded of when I am feeling weak, or afraid, or doubting whether I have changed at all.

One of my favorite things to do is belt out hymns in my car when I need to be reminded of God's goodness or provision. My family comes from a traditional Baptist background. As a young child hymns became commonplace in my life. They are packed full of truth about the greatness of God and my need for him. One of my favorites that I go back to over and over again is "Be Thou My Vision". It speaks the truth my heart needs to hear and fills the deep need for God-Mindedness in my life.

### BE THOU MY VISION

Be Thou my Vision, O Lord of my heart;
Naught be all else to me, save that Thou art.

Thou my best Thought, by day or by night,
Waking or sleeping, Thy presence my light.

Be Thou my Wisdom, and Thou my true Word;
I ever with Thee and Thou with me, Lord;
Thou my great Father, and I Thy true son;
Thou in me dwelling, and I with Thee one.

Be Thou my battle Shield, Sword for the fight;
Be Thou my Dignity, Thou my Delight;
Thou my soul's Shelter, Thou my high Tower:
Raise Thou me heav'nward, O Pow'r of my pow'r.

Riches I need not, nor man's empty praise,
Thou mine Inheritance, now and always:
Thou and Thou only, be first in my heart,
High King of Heaven, my Treasure Thou art.

High King of Heaven, my victory won,
May I reach Heav'ns joys, O bright Heaven's Sun!
Heart of my own heart, whatever befall,
Still be my Vision, O Ruler of all.

As we finish out this chapter, I want to encourage you with an important truth. **Renewing your mind will become more and more natural the more you do it.** It won't always be hard and painful. You won't always feel that crushing fear and doubt that comes with change. You won't always be this emotional. And while it seems difficult right now, the truth is this struggle is making you a stronger, more stable person. Eventually you will be free. You will be fulfilled in your life, a life with purpose and passion.

God called you to renew your mind not for His good but for YOUR good. He has taught you through His Word to be self-controlled and steady-minded so that you are able to stand. Did you know the armor of God is a great example of a person who is in the process of renewing his mind? The following scripture creates a vivid picture of renewing your mind, taking you from a person who is undefended to a person who is ready to stand and fight on the frontlines of this life, making you able to stand against the fiery darts and lies of the devil.

— *Ephesians 6:10-18*

*"Finally, be strong in the Lord and in **His mighty power.** 11 Put on the full armor of God, **so that you can take your stand** against the devil's schemes. 12 For our struggle is not against flesh and blood, but against the rulers, against the authorities, against the powers of this dark world and against the spiritual forces of evil in the heavenly realms. 13 **Therefore put on the full armor of God, so that when the day of evil comes, you may be able to stand your ground, and after you have done everything, to stand.** 14 Stand firm then, with the belt of truth buckled around your waist, with the breastplate of righteousness in place, 15 and with your feet fitted with the readiness that comes from the gospel of peace. 16 In addition to all this, take up the shield of faith, with which you can extinguish all the flaming arrows of the evil one. 17 Take the helmet of salvation and the sword of the Spirit, which is the word of God. 18 And pray in the Spirit on all occasions with all kinds of prayers and requests. **With this in mind, be alert** and always keep on praying for all the Lord's people."*

Note first that this is God's armor; it's not our own armor or in our own power. We stand in His mighty power. That is how we are able to overcome. It's interesting to note that every part of the armor of God is a piece covering the front of the body. In ancient times, the Roman armor was created so a person's front side was fully covered and protected, but their backside was completely unprotected. There was no retreat - only moving forward in the battle. Also note the description of our enemy. We are not battling against flesh and blood (people) but against spiritual enemies battling for our souls. Their entire purpose is to conquer our minds and make us ineffective in the battle.

But never forget we are in this together; you are not alone. The Roman soldiers, who had no armor protecting their backsides if surrounded, circled together with their armor facing out, so they could battle together and protect each other. Picture your battle this way. You have the armor you need to protect yourself as you advance; but if you are ever tempted to retreat, remember there are others in this battle with you. Reach out to fellow warriors and battle on!

The armor of God is all about the things we have talked about in this book. First is the belt of **TRUTH**, which holds the rest of our armor on. The breastplate of **RIGHTEOUSNESS**, thank the Lord, is the righteousness of God and not our own. Shoes of **PEACE** come from the **GOSPEL OF PEACE** or knowing our identity in view of God's grace. The shield of **FAITH** places the faith in God and not ourselves. Next comes the helmet of **SALVATION**, steadying our minds to know who we belong to and the beauty of our salvation. And finally, we take up the **SWORD OF THE SPIRIT**, the Word of God. Paul finishes this section of scripture by pointing us to the importance of **PRAYER**.

Remember this and practice these things, and you will soon be standing before the enemy victorious instead of cowering in the shadows of life. Take hold of the freedom God has given to you, and learn what it means to live a life filled with the Spirit, a life of called, victorious, and righteous purpose.

# CHAPTER SEVEN

# FIND YOUR PURPOSE

As a young girl, my ultimate life goal was to become a famous public speaker. I would be able to stand on a stage and captivate the audience by my amazing speaking skills. They would "ooh" and "aah" as I gave life-changing anecdotes and would laugh as I hit my perfect comedic timing. The problem was that I was shyer than a church mouse and wasn't very funny. However, at 12 years of age, it was my someday dream and passion for my future life. As I grew and began pursuing that dream, it became evident that my passion was just the silly dream of a little girl—or so I was told over and over again. "Who will you speak to? What will you speak to them about? How will you get people to hire you? What expertise do you bring to the table?"

As I pondered those questions, I began to doubt my purpose and calling. As an adolescent, my language regarding my future life was sure and full of promise and hope. I was confident that if God had called me to speak, He would make a way. But slowly my thinking began to shift from rock solid confidence to pretty confident and eventually to a pie-in-the-sky, never-going-to-happen type of dream. I was still passionate about speaking when I went off to Bible college, but that was just the crazy, impossible dream of a little girl. Instead, I took up the much more acceptable dream of becoming the most amazing pastor's wife and mother on the planet.

As I have had conversations with women throughout the years, this idea of "my-childhood-dream-being-shattered-and-broken-into-a-million-pieces" is much more common than you would imagine. As children, we hold the world at our fingertips and anything is possible. We believe, in our innocence, that anything is possible if I just set my mind to it and see it through. Yet as we grow, we become less and less sure of ourselves and our childhood dreams, until eventually we just give them up altogether.

For 12-year-old Britney, wanting to be a public speaker was tantamount to walking on the moon. For you, it might have been traveling the world as an adventurous archeologist or becoming a police officer, veterinarian, or firefighter. Every child naturally speaks openly and confidently about their future dreams and who they will be when they grow up. There is an air of surety when it comes to the subject of what we will be when we grow up. So why, as adults, do we shy away from our real dreams?

I spoke with a woman recently who, as a child, had a desire to open up a cupcake shop and share her passion with the world. But instead of following that dream, she ended up going to college and getting a degree in business marketing because her parents pushed her into it. She took a highly sought after, high-paying job at her father's marketing firm, and now she works 60+ hours a week. She described her job to me as "her career that was slowly sucking her life away."

When I asked her what she loved about her job, she answered me with the most depressing thing I have heard in a long time. "I don't love anything about my job, but it lets me live the life I want to live...or it will someday... hopefully." My follow-up question was the one I love to ask people when I first meet them. It is fun to see a person's eyes light up as they answer this very important inquiry: "If money was not an object, and you could do anything you wanted to do for work, what would it be?" Her answer astounded me as the words poured out of her mouth. "I love baking, specifically cupcakes. In fact, when I was young, I used to make 20 cupcakes each week and sell them door-to-door on my block. I love being creative and making something that not only tastes delicious but looks beautiful. I would love to make cupcakes for weddings and coffee shops. Wow, I haven't thought about that in many years. Oh well..." I watched her childhood excitement and passion drain from her eyes as she settled back into the responsible adult life path that had been chosen for her.

I think so often we settle for things, like this woman did, because we believe our culture: in order to be successful and have a good life, we must choose a career that is stable and makes a good income. So we settle for a life of corporate servitude and write off our purpose and calling as a childhood fantasy.

I would love to squash that idea like a bug. As we have learned in the last 6 chapters of this book, we were created for calling and purpose. The lies our culture tells us and the lies that live in our heads are exactly that...LIES. They have no power over us when we follow the principle of renewing our minds daily. We have the power to overcome the obstacles in our brain by focusing on and retraining our brain to be tuned into to the truth of God's Word.

This chapter is all about finding your passion and calling. We have laid the foundation that will help you step into this chapter and cultivate your God-calling with boldness and passion. Now we get to do the fun work of exploring and finding what it is! Before we do, here are a few Bible verses that talk about our unique calling and purpose.

### Romans 12:6-8
*"We have different gifts, according to the grace given to each of us. If your gift is prophesying, then prophesy in accordance with you faith; 7 if it is serving, then serve; if it is teaching, then teach; 8 if it is to encourage, then give encouragement; if it is giving, then give generously; if it is to lead, do it diligently; if it is to show mercy, do it cheerfully."*

### Ephesians 2:10
*"For we are God's handiwork, created in Christ Jesus to do good works, which God prepared in advance for us to do."*

### Philippians 1:6
*"Being confident of this, that he who began a good work in you will carry it on to completion until the day of Christ Jesus."*

### Ephesians 1:11
*"In him we were also chosen, having been predestined according to the plan of him who works out everything in conformity with the purpose of his will."*

# IDENTITY

Our identity in Christ directly affects our calling. If you are a part of the body of Christ and have been transformed by the Holy Spirit, then there is no doubt that God has called and equipped you for a very specific ministry/purpose to and for His glory.

There are 3 things every believer in Jesus Christ has been called to do. These are non-negotiables and are things we should consider as we investigate our purpose and calling.

1. **We are all called to share the good news of the Gospel.**
   (Matt. 28:19,20; Rom 1:16)
2. **We are all called to pray.**
   (Eph. 6:18,19; Phil. 4:4-7)
3. **We are all called to build up and encourage the body of Christ.**
   (Eph 4:6-11; Col. 3:12-15)

As we spend the rest of this chapter investigating and sorting through your dreams and passions, keep those three things in mind. Your passion and purpose should be something that has the ability, in some way, to accomplish or aid in those outcomes. The best way for you to start searching through your brain and life to find your God-calling is by asking yourself five simple questions:

## 1. WHAT IS YOUR GIFTING? ARE THERE SPECIFIC SPIRITUAL GIFTS THAT YOU HAVE?

A lot of believers have never taken the time to find out what their spiritual gifts are, and yet we all have them. I personally am gifted in apostleship (leadership), teaching, faith, and administration. There are other things that I feel God has also gifted me in, but those are the ones that I LOVE doing. It lights a fire in my soul to lead and organize a group of people. I enjoy standing up in front of a crowd of people and teaching truth from God's Word. Putting together details and planning events or organizing trips is also a passion of mine. The best part is, I don't have to work at being good at those things. They come naturally to me.

Each person who has a personal relationship with Jesus Christ has been given spiritual gifts. The purpose of spiritual gifts is to build up the Body of Christ and bring glory to God.

> ### Ephesians 4:11,12
> "So Christ himself gave the apostles, the prophets, the evangelists, the pastors and teachers, to equip his people for works of service, so that the body of Christ may be built up..."

> ### 1 Corinthians 12:27-31
> "Now you are the body of Christ, and each one of you is a part of it. 28 And God has placed in the church first of all apostles, second prophets, third teachers, then miracles, then gifts of healing, of helping, of guidance, and of different kinds of tongues. 29 Are all apostles? Are all prophets? Are all teachers? Do all work miracles? 30 Do all have gifts of healing? Do all speak in tongues? Do all interpret? 31 Now eagerly desire the greater gifts."

Just because someone has been gifted differently than you does not mean that your gifting is any less or any more important than someone else's gifts. It is interesting that the Bible describes the universal church as the BODY of believers. We are each created for a very specific purpose so that the whole body will function together just as it was created to do. In fact, the Bible very clearly lays this concept out in Romans 12.

> ### Romans 12:4-8
> *"For just as each of us has one body with many members, and these members do not all have the same function, 5 so in Christ we, though many, form one body, and each member belongs to all the others. 6 We have different gifts, according to the grace given to each of us. If your gift is prophesying, then prophesy in accordance with your faith; 7 if it is serving, then serve; if it is teaching, then teach; 8 if it is to encourage, then give encouragement; if it is giving, then give generously; if it is to lead do it diligently; if it is to show mercy, do it cheerfully."*

As people who have been created for purpose, what happens when a member of the body decides she isn't important enough to use her gifting? The picture I get in my mind is that of a person who has just stubbed her pinky toe. It's such a small part of the body and yet its purpose is vital. When you stub your pinky toe, your entire body reacts to the pain. You might even limp around for an hour or more, and your body doesn't simply forget about it. Your body never decides that it doesn't need its parts. Can you imagine if the body parts that got used less often started falling off? What would that do to your body? I know it is a gruesome picture, but it is necessary to think through the importance of your specific God-calling and gifting. Are you using it for the glory of God and to build up the church? If not, why not?

If you do not know your spiritual gifting, or this is a new concept for you, it is very simple to find out! Go online and search for "spiritual gifts test." Or better yet, if you are involved in a church, ask a mature believer or pastor to help you figure out your spiritual gifting.

**My top spiritual gifts:**

empathy/ compassion
encouragement
care Taker

## 2. WHAT MOVES YOU? WHAT ARE YOU PASSIONATE ABOUT?

We are all evangelists for something in our lives. In fact, some people are evangelists for some very weird things. For example, have you ever met a person who is so passionate about cheese that they literally smelled like a cheese cellar? You know the smell I am talking about, that not quite right, rotting but also kind of delicious smelling aroma? They talk about cheese like it is the only food worth eating in the entire world. They know exactly what wines to pair with what cheese, and they tell everyone of their expertise and passion.

My sister-in-law is passionate to help victims of sex-trafficking, so she goes out of her way to find ways to aid or raise money to help. I have another friend who is so passionate about coffee that he has devoted his entire life to it. He owns a coffee shop, roasts his own beans, and visits the coffee farms multiple times throughout the year. He takes great care in making sure that every drop of coffee he drinks or serves is extracted exactly right and is at the correct temperature. He understands at what bar pressure espresso must be extracted to make the perfect shot of espresso with just the right amount of crema. And no! you aren't the only one that doesn't understand half of those words...I'm right there with you!

Other people are evangelists for themselves. Have you ever had a conversation with a self-proclaiming ME-vangelist? In conversations where I realize I am speaking with a ME-vangelist, I like to bring up the most off-the-wall topics just to see if they will continue talking about themselves. One time, I actually had a ME-vangelist liken themselves to a slug deep in the Amazon rainforest, and then somehow made themselves out to be amazing in the process. **Every single person is an evangelist for something.** A good indication of your passion is to look at the things you talk about or are drawn to.

Now take some time to think through these questions. **What are the things that you love to talk about, or do?** If you can't think of anything, just ask your friends or family. It's usually not a hard thing to pinpoint the things that are important to a person. **What things are you passionate about? What things get your heart fluttering in the "can't wait to do that again" way?**

Worship - Music -
Bible Study -
Church -

# 3. WHAT THINGS COME EASY FOR YOU? WHAT ARE YOUR SKILLSETS AND TALENTS?

I once had a mentor tell me, "Britney, just because something is easy for you doesn't mean it's easy for everyone else." And that is true: usually our God-Calling is something that isn't terribly difficult for us to do. It is something that comes completely naturally to us. Or it is something that we love so much that we don't mind doing the hard work to accomplish it.

A really good example of this is my mom. Anyone that knows Jamie Thompson knows that she is the most happy and loving person on the planet. She can take any room and make it look like it came directly out of a magazine. She doesn't even have to have any new things in a room, and yet when she finishes, you will think she spent $1,000 on new decor. On a much deeper level, she also has the uncanny ability to make every person she meets feel loved and significant. When my mother would take us to McDonalds to play in the PlayPlace, she would often make a new friend. And not only that, she would schedule a time to have their family come to our house for dinner. She has the spiritual gift of hospitality, and it shines out of her like a light in a dark room. The thing that makes her natural talents and gifting even more impactful is her deep love for people and Jesus. It is rare to have a conversation with my mom that does not contain a spiritual aspect. Her love and care for people is in no way superficial or fake; it is genuine in every sense of the word.

This is important: your natural abilities and talents have the ability to either build you up and/or build others up. I have known many people that had the same gifting and connection with people as my mom, but they used it to manipulate and take advantage of people instead of care for and love them well. You have the same choice. **Will you use your natural abilities to pour into others or use them only for your advantage?** The truth is that when we pour out what God has naturally given us to serve others, then we reap the benefit of being filled to overflowing as well. It is like the parable of the talents as taught in Matthew 25.

> *Matthew 25:14-30*
> *"Again, it will be like a man going on a journey, who called his servants and entrusted his wealth to them. 15 To one he gave five bags of gold, to another two bags, and to another one bag, each according to his ability. Then he went on his journey. 16 The man who had received five bags of gold went at once and put his money to work and gained five bags more. 17 So also, the one with two bags of gold gained two more. 18 But the man who had received one bag went off, dug a hole in the ground and hid his master's money.*
> *19 "After a long time the master of those servants returned and settled accounts with them. 20 The man who had received five bags of gold brought the other five. 'Master,' he said, 'you entrusted me with five bags of gold. See, I have gained five more.' 21 "His master replied, 'Well done, good and faithful servant! You have been faithful with a few things; I will put you in charge of many things. Come and share your master's happiness!'*
> *22 "The man with two bags of gold also came.*

'Master,' he said, 'you entrusted me with two bags of gold; see, I have gained two more.' 23 "His master replied, 'Well done, good and faithful servant! You have been faithful with a few things; I will put you in charge of many things. Come and share your master's happiness!'

24 "Then the man who had received one bag of gold came. 'Master,' he said, 'I knew that you are a hard man, harvesting where you have not sown and gathering where you have not scattered seed. 25 So I was afraid and went out and hid your gold in the ground. See, here is what belongs to you.' 26 "His master replied, 'You wicked, lazy servant! So you knew that I harvest where I have not sown and gather where I have not scattered seed? 27 Well then, you should have put my money on deposit with the bankers, so that when I returned I would have received it back with interest.

28 "'So take the bag of gold from him and give it to the one who has ten bags.

29 For whoever has will be given more, and they will have an abundance. Whoever does not have, even what they have will be taken from them. 30 And throw that worthless servant outside, into the darkness, where there will be weeping and gnashing of teeth.' "

I find it interesting that money in this passage is the same English word as talent. This parable speaks of how we use the gifts that God has given each one of us. So often we squander or hide our natural talents, which makes this passage sobering to think about. If we don't use our talents, then they will be completely useless. What good is having these talents if we refuse to use them?

Take some time right now to write down all the things that you are naturally good at, no matter how miniscule. For example: I have the ability to find great deals on travel... like better than anyone else I know... in half the time. It is a natural talent, and it is something that brings me great satisfaction and joy. What about you? Is there anything that you can think of, even if it is seemingly insignificant, that you love to do, that makes you and others feel fulfilled and happy?

_____

_____

_____

_____

_____

## 4. ARE THERE RECURRING THEMES OR PASSIONS IN YOUR LIFE? IF SO, WHAT ARE THEY?

A God-calling that has been ignored or uncultivated has the tendency to keep popping back up over and over again. In fact, this is something that we can examine and think about on a wide scale. Think through your life. When you were six, what things did you LOVE to do? What about when you were age 10? 16? 21? 30? Etc. Did your passions change? Are there any things that have been a common thread or desire throughout your entire life?

One thing that became a recurring theme in my life was music. I LOVE MUSIC. Not only do I love listening to music, but I love singing and playing instruments. I also know that music has the ability to calm my soul when I am feeling down or discouraged. One of my favorite things to do is listen to music, dance around my house, and clean. Well, if I'm being completely honest, the cleaning part I hate. But with music the cleaning becomes tolerable.

Another recurring theme is my desire to help women get freedom in their lives. I remember being a 14-year-old in high school speaking to the guidance counselor to determine my educational path. She thought that I should pursue a career in math while I thought that I would either become a public speaker and help women overcome their struggles or become a flight attendant (because I LOVE to travel). The look of shock and disapproval on her face was priceless as she said to me, "Well, that sounds like a good dream, but what's your backup plan if that doesn't work out?"

The cool thing about your passion is that you don't need to have a backup plan. God gave you your dreams, desires, and personality for a very specific purpose. He created you to be you and ONLY you. The calling on your life will have something to do with the passions and themes in your life. Your calling is why you have those passions and dreams! **Take 5 minutes now to write down a few things that are recurring themes or passions in your life, no matter how small.**

_____

_____

_____

_____

_____

## 5. DOES IT BRING GOD GLORY? (THE MOST IMPORTANT QUESTION)

When talking about our God-calling and passion, it is important to point out that our purpose also has another more important purpose...to bring God glory! There are multiple verses in the Bible referring to the fact that God's purpose in creating us was to bring glory to Himself. **He is the only one worthy of praise, and in our God-calling and purpose, He specifically created us to bring Him the most glory we possibly can!**

> *Isaiah 43:6,7*
> *"I will say to the north, 'Give them up!'*
> *and to the south, 'Do not hold them back.'*
> *Bring my sons from afar*
> *and my daughters from the ends of the earth—*
> *7 everyone who is called by my name,*
> *whom I created for my glory,*
> *whom I formed and made."*

> *1 Corinthians 10:31*
> *"So whether you eat or drink or whatever you do,*
> *do it all for the glory of God."*

I have met people whose sole purpose is to glorify themselves. In fact, I would say most of Hollywood would very easily fit into this category. They are convinced they are the most important people in the world and all things should revolve around them. The problem with this thinking is this: that position is already taken by the all-powerful, all-knowing, all-loving, just, gracious, God of the Universe.

When we seek after our own glory and fame, our lives become so much less meaningful and purposeful. Seeking after our own happiness and fulfillment will ultimately leave us empty and wanting for more. As I said earlier, the Bible says not only were we created for His glory, we were also created to build up and encourage the Body of Christ. There is a verse in Matthew that illustrates this concept in the best way it could be said.

### Matthew 23:12

*"For those who exalt themselves will be humbled, and those who humble themselves will be exalted."*

I have seen this happen over and over in the lives of people around me in the years I worked as a full-time missionary. Being in ministry allows you to see the best and worst in people. As a 25-year-old, I saw this Bible verse play out in my own life in the most humbling way possible. I had just ended an almost-3-year relationship, and I was convinced that I could fix my shattered life on my own. In the midst of this horrible break-up, my work hours were cut down to nothing, my car was repossessed (fluke of an accident), and I had to make a move to a city where I would have to start over completely.

It was at my lowest broken point that I called out to God.

His answer was quiet at first but full of power and truth. It was like God said to me, "Are you willing to give up the control and let Me have it yet?" It was so simple! As long as I continued to put myself first, my life would never, and could never, be as good as what God had planned for me. The same is true for you. If you get to the end of this chapter and your calling and passion is all about you and your control, then we have done something wrong. God will never call us to something that does not first bring Him glory, because He is the only one worthy of ANY glory.

So now take some time to reflect and pray about this.

**Does your calling and passion bring more glory to God... or to yourself?** _____

**Is it something that will build up the body of Christ?**

_____

**Are you willing to give up control of your life to a God who never makes mistakes?** _____

# CHAPTER EIGHT

# LIVE WITH PASSION

As an 18-year-old, I was convinced that everything I desired to happen in my life would just kind of fall into place. In fact, I was so convinced I would have the perfect life that I spent very little time pursuing the things I deeply wanted out of life. I figured, hey, why not have fun while I am young. God will work out everything for my good. (A verse that I believe is misused and over quoted far too often.) So, at 18, I went to a Bible college, fell in love for the first time, got my heart shattered into a million pieces, and thought my life had fallen apart. That same month my high school best friend was killed in a car accident. I also realized I really didn't want to go to Bible college and be in full-time ministry. I was convinced that I had screwed up my entire life because it wasn't all happening exactly the way I thought it should.

At 17 years of age my plan was this: go to Bible college, fall in love, get married young, have two beautiful children that behaved perfectly, be in full-time ministry with my husband for the rest of our days, and of course travel the world. It was not a well-thought-out plan. In error, I believed life was like the romantic comedies I loved so much. You know what I am talking about, right? You know that scene in every romantic comedy where the couple's eyes meet from across the room, and from that point on they are destined to end up with one another. After one small encounter, they fall in love for all time and nothing could possibly separate them. The perfect fairy tale relationship plays out before our eyes as we sit believing, "One day my prince will come," just like the stories say. The problem is…life is messy. And those fantasies are exactly that: FANTASIES made up to make us feel good.

After my year at Bible college when all of my perfect
life dreams were broken into tiny shards, I dropped out
of college, moved home, and went through an awful
depression. I lived with my parents for the summer as I
tried to figure out how I could put the pieces of my life
back together. At the end of the summer, I moved to
Phoenix for three months in pursuit of a guy that I didn't
even like that much (YES! I WAS DESPERATE…no
judging, okay?) And three months later I got my heart
broken again.

I am not telling you all of this to make you feel sorry
for me but to help you realize that I didn't just end up
where I am today by coincidence. It took many years of
immaturity, hurts, heartbreak, an eating disorder, a called-
off engagement in my mid-20's, being emotionally and
verbally abused, and a few moves back home to Utah to
finally be ready to pursue my God-calling fully. And,
through it all, God was "working everything together for
my good." Yes, even those things in your life you wish you
could hide from the world forever are for your good. I can
honestly say that without all the hurt and difficulty, I don't
think I would be the same confident, called, woman of God
I am today.

I thank the Lord every day He didn't give me what I
thought I wanted when I was 18 because, honestly, I had
no idea what I wanted or even who I really was at 18.
How about you? Now, as a single 35-year-old woman, I
am still reminded often (by other people), "SOMEDAY
you will meet your Prince Charming." But I don't think
that's a promise God has made to me. In fact, there is a
chance I may never meet and marry the Godly Christian

man I desire; and I am okay with that. God has promised amazing things in His Word that we can know with certainty He has ready for us. But He has never promised our lives will work out exactly the way we hope and dream they will.

All of that to say, life is messy, and your passions are 100% worth pursuing even when your life is not working out the way you had hoped it would. This chapter is all about that: pursuing your God-calling in the midst of the unpredictability that is life. Pursuing your God-calling probably won't be easy, it will most definitely be messy, but it will also be worth it.

We spent the last chapter honing in on the things you are passionate about. Our passions are a huge factor in the calling God has put on our lives. Our skillsets, opportunities, and spiritual gifting, mixed with our passions, make up the base for our God-calling. Now we get to use all of those things to pursue our call and our God to our fullest capacity!

As you have read through this book, I am sure you have figured out what my passion and calling is. But in case it's unclear, here it is!

I have been called by God to help women break free from the lies in their heads so that they are able to step into their God-calling with purpose and passion. Through writing, speaking, and one-on-one discipleship I get to help women BELIEVE WHO God SAYS THEY ARE and fully step into their calling! How cool is that?

Now it's your turn! Take what you have learned and move toward making it a reality. It probably won't turn out exactly the way you think it should, but God's plan is so much better than ours. All God asks of us is that we trust Him and follow His leading.

**Proverbs 16:9**
*"In their hearts humans plan their course, but the LORD establishes their steps."*

**Psalm 32:8**
*"I will instruct you and teach you in the way you should go; I will counsel you with my loving eye on you."*

**Proverbs 3:5,6**
*"Trust in the LORD with all your heart and lean not on your own understanding; 6 in all your ways submit to him, and he will make your paths straight."*

You may be thinking at this point, "How in the world do I start pursuing my calling? I'm nobody special. I live in a tiny podunk town in the middle of nowhere. How can God possibly use me to affect change in the world?" I get it girl; that is my story, too. I grew up in a town of 6,000 people in the center of Utah. Not only was I called to help women get freedom in their lives and follow their God-calling, but I believed God was calling me to share the message from a stage, to thousands of people. God was calling me to turn the world upside down for His glory. So I started small; in fact I'm still starting small, just taking one step at a time, knowing that if God is in it and has called me to this, it will not fail. Am I scared? Absolutely! Do I doubt that I heard

His calling correctly? Sometimes, when my own insecurity creeps in. But am I doing what I love for the glory of God with everything in me? YES! 100% YES!

That's all it takes, a willingness to be used by a God who desires to use YOU to bring Him glory. So let's dive in to what it takes to start pursuing your life purpose.

# 1. COMPILE YOUR LIST OF NON-NEGOTIABLES.

This is important, since we as human beings have a tendency to overdo things at times. There are things in your life that are 100% worth fighting for, things that you MUST have in your life to feel like a sane human being. These are the things that may not have much to do with your calling but have everything to do with being a normal functioning member of society and a called and devoted follower of Jesus.

I know too many people who start pursuing their calling and within a few years they are walking away because "it was just too much work" or "it took more time and energy than I thought." What these people didn't do was set up protective barriers for their life and ministry. For example, these are my non-negotiables:

1. **I will not work more than 50 hours a week total. That includes any income opportunities and pursuing my God-calling.**
2. **I will take one full day off for rest and relaxation every week.**
3. **I will take time to be with my family often.**

4. I will not overfill my life with busyness just because I am called to serve God and the body of Christ.

5. I will put God first over my life purpose and calling. (Sounds logical, but you would be surprised how often I try to do it in my own strength.)

6. I will travel out of the country at least once a year for vacation.

7. I will not start my work day until I have been able to pray and get into God's Word.

8. I will have women in my life to whom I am accountable, who have permission to be totally honest with me no matter what.

These are my non-negotiables. These are things that are so important to me that they come even before I begin pursuing my calling. These things make me able to fully pursue and implement my God-calling every day in the healthiest way possible. They will stop me from getting to the point of burn out, if they are in place. You also need to have these things in place in your own life. Whether or not this book spurs you on to pursue your God-calling and be a world changer for the glory of God, I hope it makes you look at your life from a different perspective. A wonderful series by Andy Stanley called, "Guardrails," talks about setting up boundaries in your life and ministry. I highly recommend watching it as you figure out what your non-negotiables are for your life.

We were never meant to live our lives in a constant state of busyness and being overwhelmed. If that describes your life, it's time to stop and take a breather. Within the past two years, I have cut out many of the non-important activities in my life. I have worked hard to make the main thing the main thing and said "no" to good opportunities in order to pursue the things that bring me the most joy and give God the most glory.

## 2. HOW DO YOUR DREAMS AND PASSION FIT INTO YOUR LIFE?

This goes without saying, but God has placed you where you are for a specific purpose. While I could probably minister to young mothers and teach parenting classes, it's just not something that is in my wheelhouse or even a part of my life at this moment in time. And for those of you that are in those early mothering years, I have a feeling that packing up everything you own in your Prius and making a 12-month trek across the country probably isn't a good use of your time and resources right now. But for me, as a single woman with nothing tying me down, it's the perfect time!

If God has called you to something that is beyond your capacity at this moment in time, do not fret. The Bible is full of people who were called years before they ever got to get their hands dirty pursuing their purpose.

Look at Moses as an example. From birth, it's clear God has called him for a very specific purpose. He goes through his formative years in the Pharaoh's palace, eventually commits murder and then runs away. Great start, huh? As he is living in the land of Midian, God calls him from the burning bush to lead the Israelites out of their Egyptian captivity. God calls a murdering run-away to be the leader of the Israelite nation for the next 40+ years - amazing! But that calling started far before Moses' encounter with God at the burning bush. It started the moment he was born. He was born for a specific purpose and calling; and almost 80 years later he was able to step into that calling fully. Did you catch that? Moses was 80 years old when his life purpose came to fruition.

Or how about the example of Joseph? As a young boy he was already seeing dreams and visions of his purpose and calling in the future. But first he had to be thrown into a pit, sold into slavery, be falsely accused by Potiphar's wife, spend 2+ years in prison, interpret the dreams of the cup-bearer, and interpret Pharaoh's dream, before he became the most powerful advisor of Egypt and was able to store up grain for the famine. Because of God's hand on Joseph's life, Joseph's father and all his brothers would be saved by making a move to Egypt. Then, four hundred years later, Moses would be the one called by God to lead the people of Israel back to their homeland. Isn't God's plan just amazing?

My story and calling are unique and different, just like yours is. For me, it's been over 20 years of God's calling on my life to get me to the place where I can fully pursue it. For you, it may be five years down the road…or next week. But the truth is, God's plan for your life cannot be thwarted by your life circumstances or random acts of stupidity. He will accomplish His purpose in your life in His perfect timing, whether it's now or 40 years down the road! God has placed you exactly where you are, at this exact moment in time, because you can affect change there better than anyone else can. Believe it, girl!

## 3. START EXACTLY WHERE YOU ARE.

Where you are right now is the perfect place to start. You don't have to know all of the information or have a plan for the next 10 years into the future; you just need to start taking small, actionable steps toward your purpose. If you are passionate about homeless ministry, start volunteering at the rescue mission nearest to you. Or you could put together little care packages to hand out and start getting acquainted with the homeless population in your area. Do you feel led to reach inner city youth for Jesus? Start meeting them. Volunteer at their schools or join a big brother/big sister program. Start an afternoon pick-up ball game in their neighborhood and invite them to join. Do you feel called to help victims of human trafficking? Start reaching out to organizations that already do that and find out how you can get involved. Maybe you have a desire to make senior citizens feel special and loved. Start visiting them and playing games with them.

Wherever you are now, you can begin pursuing your God-calling by taking a step of faith in that direction. The nice thing about starting small is that you get to grow with your ministry or calling, and God is the one who will be guiding and directing each step you take. For two years now, I have been actively and passionately pursuing my calling. I have written a book, begun to grow a following, built a website, created a Bible study guide, started speaking at local churches and events, and hosted a few women's retreats. I am currently getting ready to take my ministry full-time by going on the road for the next year to connect with churches and women's ministry leaders across the

US. And the funny thing is, if my original plan (to get married young) would have worked out, I would not be able to pursue this ministry as fully as I get to right now. As a single woman, I am perfectly set up to be a traveling, homeless nomad for the next year of my life.

So where can you start? Take 5 minutes right now to jot down a couple of ideas of where to start. Think small... in fact the smaller the better. I once heard that if a person created a list of small goals that led to the completion of one large goal, they are more likely to finish it than if they would have just created one big goal and tried to complete it all at once. Here is an example from my own life.

I want to build an online community of women world changers who can support, encourage, and love one another while pursuing their God-calling. I want it to be thousands of women strong, and I want it to be a resource that will give women the ability to communicate and connect worldwide. THAT IS A HUGE GOAL. So I have broken it down into smaller actionable steps.

1. *Start an online community group.*
2. *Create a mini video series about renewing your mind; offer it free on my website.*
3. *Create an online program that will walk through the principles taught in God-Minded. Offer it to the people who have watched the free series.*
4. *Give lifetime access to anyone who purchases the program.*
5. *Create unique opportunities for women to connect with one another inside of the group.*
6. *Watch it grow over time.*

Some of those steps are bigger than others, but in about 10 years, I may see that original BIG goal come to fruition through those smaller, much more manageable, and less overwhelming goals. Each one of those smaller steps brings me one step closer to the end goal, but I am not feeling like I have to start at the end point. I am starting with the smallest step possible, knowing that it will bring me one step closer to reaching that big goal. You can do that same thing. I believe in you. Now it's time to believe God's purpose for your life.

I would also like to remind you about that little lie of perfection we so often believe. The lie is this: you can't start taking those small steps until you have the BIG plan perfectly thought out and in place. That lie will keep you stuck EXACTLY where you are right now. A coach told me something done at 70% will get done and still be fun, but something done at 100% will stress you out and be no fun at all. It's true. We have not been called to perfection but to progress and obedience. I have a friend that recently started an Etsy shop. She creates digital downloads and does pretty well at it, too. When she started, she had just a few things listed on her shop. Now, as her business grows, she adds to her body of work, and her shop is becoming more and more full of designs. But what if she would have waited until ALL of her designs were ready before she launched her business? She would still be waiting. She wouldn't have started at all. **Perfection is a lie that keeps us from moving forward, and it's a lie that our brains are masterful at using.** Don't let perfection hold you back from taking the first steps toward your God-calling.

***Start today!***

# 4. MAKE TIME IN YOUR SCHEDULE NOW.

As I have coached and spoken to women over the
years, I have many say to me, "Someday I want to
_____." They talk about it as though
they are waiting for their life to finally begin once they
are done living the life they feel like they must live first:
the responsible, no fun, unfulfilled life of a citizen of the
United States. The truth is that each one of us has only 24
hours in a day. So what is the difference between a person
pursuing their calling and passion and a person who is just
living life to get to that point where they can finally live life
the way they want?

The difference is simple. They don't believe what God
says about them. They have bought into the lie that they
must fulfill all of life's obligations before they can finally
begin to live. Do we see those principles taught anywhere
in scripture? I don't believe so, and in fact I think exactly
the opposite is taught.

> *Matthew 6:25-34*
> *"Therefore I tell you, do not be anxious about your
> life, what you will eat or what you will drink, nor
> about your body, what you will put on. Is not life more
> than food, and the body more than clothing? 26 Look
> at the birds of the air: they neither sow nor reap nor
> gather into barns, and yet your heavenly Father feeds
> them. Are you not of more value than they? 27 And
> which of you by being anxious can add a single hour
> to his span of life? 28 And why are you anxious about
> clothing? Consider the lilies of the field, how they*

*grow: they neither toil nor spin, 29 yet I tell you, even Solomon in all his glory was not arrayed like one of these. 30 But if God so clothes the grass of the field, which today is alive and tomorrow is thrown into the oven, will he not much more clothe you, O you of little faith? 31 Therefore do not be anxious, saying, 'What shall we eat?' or 'What shall we drink?' or 'What shall we wear?' 32 For the Gentiles seek after all these things, and your heavenly Father knows that you need them all. 33 But seek first the kingdom of God and his righteousness, and all these things will be added to you. 34 "Therefore do not be anxious about tomorrow, for tomorrow will be anxious for itself. Sufficient for the day is its own trouble."*

*Luke 12:16-21*

*"And he told them this parable: "The ground of a certain rich man yielded an abundant harvest. 17 He thought to himself, 'What shall I do? I have no place to store my crops.' 18 "Then he said, 'This is what I'll do. I will tear down my barns and build bigger ones, and there I will store my surplus grain. 19 And I'll say to myself, "You have plenty of grain laid up for many years. Take life easy; eat, drink and be merry."'*
*20 "But God said to him, 'You fool! This very night your life will be demanded from you. Then who will get what you have prepared for yourself?'*
*21 "This is how it will be with whoever stores up things for themselves but is not rich toward God."*

I am in no way saying that saving and thinking about the future is a bad thing. I just believe these stories and parables teach us something more about life. We were never meant to live for the future. The Bible talks over and over again about living life fully and abundantly; not living in the future, but living fully and completely in the present.

A story in the Bible stands out to me and is played out over and over again through multiple broken individuals all throughout scripture. But this one instance is so full of God's glory and so evident of man's brokenness that I want to share it with you.

seraphim

*Isaiah 6:1-8*
*"In the year that King Uzziah died, I saw the Lord seated on a throne, high and exalted; and the train of His robe filled the temple. 2 Above Him stood seraphim, each having six wings: With two wings they covered their faces, with two they covered their feet, and with two they were flying. 3 And they were calling out to one another:*
        *"Holy, holy, holy is the LORD of Hosts;*
        *all the earth is full of His glory."*
*4 At the sound of their voices the doorposts and thresholds shook, and the temple was filled with smoke. 5 Then I said:*
        *"Woe is me,*
        *for I am ruined,*
        *because I am a man of unclean lips*
        *dwelling among a people of unclean lips;*
        *for my eyes have seen the King,*
        *the LORD of Hosts."*
*6 Then one of the seraphim flew to me, and in his hand was a glowing coal that he had taken with tongs from the altar. 7 And with it he touched my mouth and said:*

*"Now that this has touched your lips,*
*your iniquity is removed*
*and your sin is atoned for."*
8 *Then I heard the voice of the Lord saying:*
*"Whom shall I send?*
*Who will go for Us?"*
*And I said:*
*"Here am I. Send me!""*

I just love the range of raw emotion and awe from Isaiah in this passage. First, can you imagine visiting the throne room of God? Secondly, he realizes he is not worthy to stand in the presence of this Holy God. He is undone by God's glory. In the next moment, his sins are washed clean, and he is able to answer the question God asks: "Whom shall I send? Who will go for Us?" And I love Isaiah's response: "Here am I, send me." Not only does he realize he is exactly the person for the job, but he willingly steps into this calling at that very moment. And what a difficult calling it was. God called Isaiah to speak the truth of God to people who would not hear his words. He called him to speak words of destruction over the wayward nation of Israel. Aren't you glad that's not your calling?

Throughout scripture we see called people doing what they were called to do, sometimes with gritted teeth. Take Jonah for instance: he was called by God to preach repentance to Nineveh. Instead he ran away; so God got his attention by chasing him down and having a big fish swallow him. Then, when he finally did heed the call of God and preach to Nineveh, he was upset that the people of Nineveh repented. We scoff at Jonah's story sometimes, but how often is that our own story?

**Messy people, unclean people, and unqualified people are the people God chooses to accomplish His purpose in this world.** The insecurity you are feeling about reaching out to your next door neighbor or about that wayward youth art class you want to start is totally normal. In fact, I don't think you would be human if there wasn't some apprehension, fear, and insecurity that comes up when you think about stepping into your God-calling. Don't let that hold you back from the thing that will bring you the most joy and the most fulfillment in life.

Can I tell you a secret? I am also afraid. I also doubt my ability. I also wonder if I will fail. Every person on the planet deals with those feelings and emotions that come up when big changes are happening. **The difference between a person who is successful and a person who stays comfortable and stuck in their life is their ability to feel fear, push past it and accomplish their goals anyway.** Fear and doubt are an inevitable part of life. But the good news is that we were never called to overcome it alone.

I would like to end this chapter and this book with a declaration over your life, not because of who you are but because of who God is and has said you are. Your life calling and purpose has very little to do with your own efforts and has everything to do with who God created you to be and with what He will accomplish through you. God's faithfulness is the most faithful. His plan will not be unraveled. His works are better than ours by far. He can finish what He started in you. All He asks from you is simple obedience.

**God's plan and calling for your life are unique to you.**
There will never be another you on this planet. He knew
what He was doing when He created every inch of your
body and every hair on your head. He knew what talents
and skills you would have. He understands how your
mind works. He sees your weaknesses, fear, doubt, and
insecurity, and chooses to use you anyway. He knows what
sins you have hidden away in your closet; and if you are in
Christ, He has forgiven them all. You don't have to have
a college degree, or be a wife and mother, or do something
extra special to fulfill the call of God on your life. You are
not required to walk out your purpose perfectly. You are
only called to obedience. And through that obedience to
God's perfect, loving call, you will live a life of purpose
and passion.

*This is the life you were created to live.*

165

A Puritan prayer from the book "The Valley of Vision":

*O God, most high, most glorious, the thought of Your infinite serenity cheers me, for I am toiling and moiling, troubled and distressed, but You are forever at perfect peace. Your designs cause You no fear or care of unfulfillment; they stand fast as the eternal hills. Your power knows no bond, Your goodness no stint. You bring order out of confusion, and my defeats are Your victories: The Lord God omnipotent reigneth.*

*I come to You as a sinner with cares and sorrows, to leave every concern entirely to You, every sin calling for Christ's precious blood; revive deep spirituality in my heart; let me live near to the great Shepherd, hear His voice, know its tones, follow its calls. Keep me from deception by causing me to abide in the truth, from harm by helping me to walk in the power of the Spirit. Give me intenser faith in the eternal verities, burning into me by experience the things I know; Let me never be ashamed of the truth of the Gospel, that I may bear its reproach, vindicate it, see Jesus as its essence, know in it the power of the Spirit.*

*Lord, help me, for I am often lukewarm and chill; unbelief mars my confidence, sin makes me forget You. Let the weeds that grow in my soul be cut at their roots; grant me to know that I truly live only when I live to You, that all else is trifling. Your presence alone can make me holy, devout, strong and happy. Abide in me, gracious God.*

# ACKNOWLEDGEMENTS

I would just like to take some time right now to sincerely thank the women who poured their time and energy into this project. It was by no means a one woman show. I cannot tell you how many hours were spent in conversation and reflection over the contents of this book.

*TEREASA,* thank you for your experience and expertise in editing and making this book readable and grammatically correct. You are an amazing friend and co-laborer in the Gospel.

*NAOMI,* thank you for your insight and support of this project. Your contribution to this work is such a beautiful testament to the power of renewing your mind. Thank you for being faithful to the call of God on your life.

*BECKI,* I cherish the hours we spent over the phone talking through God-Minded. Your insight and wisdom spoke truth when I needed to hear it most. I honestly don't know if I could have done this without your loving support.

*GRANDMA,* thank you for making sure my book is the best it can be. Thanks for the hours of conversations, grammar lessons and coffee.

*AND FINALLY,* to the godly, AMAZING, women who have read my book and given me life-giving feedback and support THANK YOU. You are my favorite women in this whole world!

# GOD-MINDED
## ONLINE COURSE

God-Minded online course will walk you through the process of renewing your mind in just six weeks. Britney will be there to guide you each step of the way with teaching, live coaching, accountability, and support.

*Launching Spring of 2020.*

# GOD-MINDED
## one - on - one

God-Minded one-on-one is an online mastermind coaching program that allows you to dig deep with Britney for six full weeks.

*Launching Summer of 2020*

# GOD-MINDED *Retreat*

God-Minded Retreat is a live event that will be three full days of teaching, fellowship, worship, relaxation and fun. Limit 30 attendees. Travel expenses not inlcuded.

*Registration opens late Spring of 2020*

Made in the USA
Columbia, SC
22 December 2019